MANDELL CREIGHTON
AND THE ENGLISH CHURCH

MANDELL CREIGHTON, 1899

an unfinished portrait by Herkomer
in the possession of Mr. Hugh Creighton

Mandell Creighton and the English Church

BY

W. G. FALLOWS

Principal of Ripon Hall, Oxford
Chaplain to the Queen

London
OXFORD UNIVERSITY PRESS
NEW YORK   TORONTO
1964

Oxford University Press, Amen House, London E.C.4

GLASGOW NEW YORK TORONTO MELBOURNE WELLINGTON
BOMBAY CALCUTTA MADRAS KARACHI LAHORE DACCA
CAPE TOWN SALISBURY NAIROBI IBADAN ACCRA
KUALA LUMPUR HONG KONG

Printed in Great Britain by
The Camelot Press Ltd., London and Southampton

PREFACE

MANDELL CREIGHTON, historian, and bishop successively of Peterborough and London, died on 14 January 1901, eleven days before Queen Victoria. He was only fifty-seven and at the height of his powers. Today he is best remembered in the world of scholarship as the historian of the Papacy, but he was no less distinguished as an ecclesiastical statesman and especially as an interpreter of the character and mission of the Church of England. It is this latter aspect of his work that this short study seeks to underline.

Many of the current issues of church polity, great and small, are illustrated by one aspect or another of the teaching and episcopal administration of Mandell Creighton. Questions of marriage discipline, of Canon Law, of relations with other churches, of the Holy Communion, and of the role of the Church in the life of the nation—all these and many another question of the present day were matters on which Creighton, with his unrivalled historical knowledge, made wise and penetrating judgements that are relevant today. Some of his conclusions, especially, perhaps, on the ritual controversies, will no doubt seem 'dated' in the more eirenic and ecumenical atmosphere of the present day. So, too, his ardent nationalism may have been the cause of some confusion in his own mind on the link between the Church and the nation. Nevertheless, his views on the Church and State relationship are specially significant for the present time.

Institutional religion is at a low ebb and the Church of England has shared in the general decline. Its influence on the life of the nation is nothing like so powerful or beneficial as Creighton believed it to be. If it is to recover and be the nation on its spiritual side it will only be as it re-discovers the basis of its own life and position in Christendom. In this return to the roots Mandell Creighton is a guide whom the present-day churchman can profitably recall.

Creighton's widow wrote a superb biography of her husband, published in two volumes in 1904. J. N. Figgis described it as one of the six best biographies in the English language. I have no idea what were the other five he had in mind and the practice of weighing books on the scales is, perhaps, best left to the Desert Island Quiz. But by any standard it is a great book and the reader who wishes to know Creighton in depth must work his way through the meandering by-ways of this most rewarding biography. It is not now easily obtainable and has long been out of print. Nor is ours a generation that is likely to return to the massive two-volume biographies which the Victorians laid like funeral wreaths on the graves of their worthies. For this reason, among others, a shorter study of Creighton is needed if his message is to be heard by the present generation of English churchmen.

In addition to her massive biography, Mrs. Creighton also published most of her husband's lectures, charges, and addresses. These have all been drawn on freely in the present study. Through the kindness of the late Mrs. Cyril Bailey, the youngest daughter of Mandell Creighton, I was able to make use of a number of manuscript appreciations of Creighton written by his contemporaries, and also to read through the copious notebooks prepared by Mrs. Creighton in connexion with her biography of her husband. I shall ever be grateful for this privilege and for the hospitality I enjoyed while engaged on such a congenial task. My thanks are also due to Mr. Hugh Creighton for permission to reproduce a portrait of his grand-father now in his possession, and to Mrs. H. E. Westall for much valued help in preparing the typescript of this book.

W. G. FALLOWS.

Ripon Hall,
Oxford, 1963.

CONTENTS

1 · LIFE IN OUTLINE

MANDELL CREIGHTON, the son of a carpenter, was born at Carlisle on 5 July 1843. His father, Robert Creighton, Mayor of Carlisle in 1866, enjoyed a considerable reputation in the northern city, where he extended a family business in a shop opposite the Cathedral. Here Mandell Creighton spent his early years in an austere household. His mother, Sarah, was the tenth child of Thomas Mandell, a yeoman farmer from Bolton, Cumberland. She died when Mandell, her eldest child, was seven.

Robert Creighton, who never married again, was reserved, hard-working, and strongly attached to his liberal principles. The household in which Mandell Creighton grew up was well ordered, but it lacked any stimulus of literary and artistic interest. Nor was there much outward show of affection. There was a strong sense of duty; the children were expected to have their heads screwed on the right way. No doubt Mandell Creighton absorbed some of his father's liberal principles, but there was no paternal encouragement in the fields of literature, architecture, and history, in which he was later to distinguish himself.

From the Cathedral School in Carlisle, Creighton went to Durham School, where he made rapid progress and became head boy. He was nicknamed 'Homer', a tribute to his ability to construe. Already short-sighted, he showed no proficiency at games. Walking was his chief recreation from childhood to the end of his life.

His religious life was nurtured by the Durham Cathedral services rather than by any influence of the school. Nor was there any strong religious influence at home. In matters of faith and devotion, Creighton had to find his own feet. His spiritual self-dependence stood him in good stead in later years, when so many in perplexity, in personal distress, in spiritual and intellectual difficulties appealed to him for guidance and help.

The steps by which he secured his firm hold on the Christian faith are not disclosed. Creighton was reticent about his own spiritual development. The absence of any marked religious influence at home may be the reason why there was no period of religious rebellion and doubt so common among lively young minds. Although he possessed an acute and critical intelligence, he does not seem to have been disturbed by the great religious controversies of his time. He was not influenced by anyone in particular in his decision to be ordained—a decision which disappointed his father, although he took no steps to frustrate it.

The young are gay and grave: their gaiety is not surprising; their gravity sometimes passes comprehension. One of the most solemn letters that can ever have been written by a boy of his age came from the pen of Mandell Creighton in the year 1864, shortly after he had been head of Durham School. Two thousand words in length, it is addressed to a friend who had succeeded him as head of the school: 'I am going to take the liberty of writing a few observations on the duties of the monitors and the best way of fulfilling them. . . . You will excuse me if I say that I think you need it; you are all of you still young to be monitors.'[1] There is not much about their duties and the manner of fulfilling them which they do not know when they have persevered to the end of Mandell Creighton's epistolary lecture. A monitor has to set the moral tone of the school. 'Every glance of the eye is a blessing or a curse to every one on whom it falls.'[2] Nothing of which the monitor's conscience disapproves must go unrebuked, nor must the monitor be influenced by pity for the offender, but rather he must consider the immense harm that may be done to others if the culprit is allowed to go on unchecked. Filthy talk and all indecency are the greatest perils that beset a school. Frequenting public houses (an especial temptation in the football season) must be stamped out. 'As regards punishment, I strongly recommend giving a fellow a thrashing, the fellows like it best themselves . . . and remember never thrash a fellow a *little*, always *hard*.'[3]

These are but a few of the young man's monitions to the monitors of Durham School. 'And now, if you ask me *how* you are to do all this, I am sure you will all feel where the best help is to be found; also you will find a frequent attendance at the Holy Communion a very great assistance to you indeed.'[4] The child is father of the man.

But of what kind of man is this youth the father? Is this 'Pastoral', as the letter was always called in the Creighton household, a portent of a prig or a pastor? There is no doubt about the answer. For all its gravity, there is no trace of the sanctimonious in the youthful Creighton's laboured moral lecture. 'Was there ever such a letter', says Scott Holland 'written at such an age? It has in it the earnest wisdom of the man who has thought everything out. . . . It is an amazing letter, and exhibits the sincerity and force of his inherent bent towards the philosophy of moral conduct, even when a boy.'[5]

In 1862 Creighton gained a classical postmastership at Merton College, Oxford. Caird, afterwards Master of Balliol, was his tutor for 'Greats' and said of him: 'Creighton possesses common sense in a degree which amounts to genius.' His facility for rapid and concentrated work left him some time for other pursuits. A founder member of the Merton College Whist Club, he also found diversion in rowing, but his chief recreation and delight was walking. Once he walked from Oxford to Durham to attend the school Speech Day.

As an undergraduate Creighton was a definite high churchman, observing the fasts and absenting himself from dinner in Hall on Fridays. He was one of a small circle of kindred spirits who took tea in each other's rooms and read aloud St. Augustine's *Confessions*. He enjoyed the best of Oxford: long walks, long talks, and hard and steady reading. The path of life ran smoothly and the results were commensurate with his ability and effort; a first in 'Mods', a first in 'Greats', and, after six months' reading, a second in Law and History. A first in so short a time would have shaken his confidence in the History School. Elected a Fellow of Merton in December 1866, he settled down to academic life, turning more and more to historical work and lecturing chiefly on ecclesiastical, Italian, and Byzantine history.

Ordination followed in due course, as Deacon in 1870 and as Priest in 1873. The casualness of the ordination arrangements is a reflection of the laxity still prevalent in the eighteen-seventies, in spite of a generation of the Oxford Movement and four decades of liberal reform. Creighton saw nothing of the Bishop of Oxford (Dr. Mackarness) before ordination and was not required to spend any time at Cuddesdon before his ordination as Deacon or Priest. He was nervous and disconsolate over the priest's examination and went to Archdeacon Palmer (one of the examining chaplains) to withdraw his name. It cannot have been difficult for the Archdeacon to give the necessary reassurance to the candidate who was destined to become one of the front-rank historical scholars of his age and one of the ablest bishops of his generation.

In 1872, between his ordination as Deacon and his ordination as Priest, Creighton married Louise Von Glehn, the youngest daughter of Robert Von Glehn, a London merchant who hailed from Reval in the Russian Baltic Provinces. Their courtship had been largely spent looking at pictures in the National Gallery, and Kensington Museum, and in studying early Italian engravings in the Print Room of the British Museum. Creighton taught his fiancée Italian; she in turn helped him with German. Each was a good match for the other, sharing intellectual interests, possessing strong personalities. Shortly after the wedding Creighton wrote to his wife: 'Remember I will never give way to you in my views, but will teach you tolerance first, and then we will convince one another gradually.' Thus began a domestic partnership which was a continued source of strength and solace to Creighton to the end of his days. A harmony of outlook and ideals reigned between them.

Merton had passed a special statute to enable four college fellows to marry without forfeiting their fellowships. The immediate purpose was to retain Creighton and for a few years longer he continued to enjoy the life of a don. It was a smooth and easy life with no great worries. He writes in 1874: 'Up to the present time I have found life tolerably cheerful. I have learnt that when one can't get what one wants, one can at least leave off wanting it. I have learnt that what is, is best, that regrets are quite useless, that life in the present and future alone is useful for man: that no one need ever be disappointed or even seriously annoyed unless he chooses: cares may come and knock at the door, but the fault lies with him who is fool enough to open it.' Life was very serene for the newly-married Oxford don who enjoyed his teaching and his studies. The present was peaceful and the future as distant as it was unknown. But though life at Oxford was overflowing with contentment for the scholar and the teacher it was not large enough to satisfy his other gifts. The University was too narrow a field for his energy and practical ability. The turning-point came when he was offered the living of Embleton, in Northumberland.

VICAR OF EMBLETON

His own college, Merton, were the patrons. The parish was a large and scattered country district stretching for some miles along the Northumberland coast. In itself it was no light task; there were four schools and a population of about sixteen hundred concentrated in several centres. Many of his academic friends and colleagues were disappointed when Creighton decided to accept the living. They were dubious of his wisdom and thought his move was self-appointed banishment.

Events were to prove that Creighton was right in his decision. Parish work brought him into fuller and closer contact with human life; it developed sympathies and powers which, though partly latent at Oxford, proved some of the strongest elements in his influence. So in the Christmas vacation of 1874 the Creighton household moved to the imposing, if somewhat austere, Vicarage at Embleton. On the way Creighton called at Bishop Auckland. He found the Bishop (Baring) a kindly old gentleman who objected to ritualists on principle, but was essentially pacific by nature. A natural gossip, he knew about everybody in his diocese, but, to Creighton's surprise, made no inquiry about Creighton's views or intentions.

The new wallpapers in a modernist vein for the Vicarage and Creighton's liberal political views resulted in an element of self-restraint in the brotherly welcome accorded to him by the neighbouring clergy, and there was some suspicion among his Northumberland parishioners. But he threw himself into the work of the parish with energy and devotion. He made a point of knowing everyone in the parish and visited them diligently. He instituted services in two of the more distant villages. Twice a Sunday he preached simple and ethical sermons. His object in preaching was first to give an accurate account of the facts and statements of Scripture and then, secondly, to impress some practical lesson. He was on intimate terms with the leading families of the district, especially the Greys of Howick and Falloden. The years at Embleton were the golden years and the happiest years. It was here that much of the work was completed for his five-volume *History of the Papacy*. The instincts of the student and the pastor were given full range. But far from being the scholarly recluse and country parson, Creighton also took an active part in local government and soon became immersed in the public life of the county as Chairman of the Board of Guardians and of the School Attendance Committee.

On the ecclesiastical front, too, more and more calls were made upon him. Bishop Baring had allowed the office of Rural Dean to lapse when a holder of it died. When Lightfoot succeeded Baring as Bishop of Durham he filled the vacant deaneries and appointed Creighton Rural Dean of Alnwick. The diocese of Newcastle was created during Creighton's incumbency of Embleton. As one of the more prominent incumbents in the new diocese Creighton had to carry his share of the work of money-raising and organization. Thus the scholar-parson kept his feet on the ground and, though often he would rather be back at his books than attending committees in Newcastle, he was gaining first-hand experience of the machinery of civil and ecclesiastical organization. Meanwhile, there was no slackening in his academic pursuits. His versatility

combined with his energy enabled him to keep many pots on
the boil. He lectured frequently on historical and literary
subjects and persevered with his main historical work on the
Papacy. The first two volumes appeared in 1882 and established his reputation as a historian.

Immersed though he was in public duties and literary
labours, it was his pastoral work that made his life at Embleton
so serene and happy. Creighton was not one of those clergymen
who find relief from their primary tasks by escaping into the
world of committees. Enjoyable as were his social intimacies
with the county families, he confesses without affectation or in-
sincerity that the love of simple souls, who taught him more
than he taught them, was his chief delight. So, too, it was in
contact with children, with the young, the sorrowful, and the
tempted that his own sympathies grew and the Embleton years
became formative in his own development.

The parochial mission, a common feature of the Victorian
religious scene, found no favour with Creighton, in spite of his
pastoral concern for the spiritual welfare of the parish.
'Missions', he writes, 'are a mistake from our point of view.
They tend to keep up the popular belief in emotional states of
mind being of any serious value. It seems to me that man wants
as the basis of his personal religion a rational conviction of the
need of a spiritual side to his life. Missions obscure this truth;
they appeal to a man's terror or superstitions and they create
something which is evanescent in most cases.'[6] So there was no
beating of the drum or distribution of decision cards or special
evangelistic campaigns in the parish of Embleton.

One of the secrets of Creighton's many-sided achievements
there, as historian, lecturer, diocesan official, parish priest, and
public figure, was his capacity for economizing in time and dis-
regarding interruptions. There are no office hours in a parson's
life and no rigid time-table. He cannot be shielded from interruptions, and if he has literary ambitions that involve tedious
and concentrated research he must always be ready to have the
thread of his concentration broken and his seclusion invaded.
Creighton would often be interrupted in his work by one of the

pupils whom he had staying at the Vicarage from time to time. Frequently a parishioner would call when he was in the thick of his Papacy studies. No matter how trivial the call might be he would lay down his pen ungrudgingly, give himself to whatever was wanted of him, and then return to his work without effort. Another secret of his success was his ability to use odd scraps of time for some serious and profitable purpose. He was drawing upon his own example and experience of these years when, in the last year of his life, he told the members of the London Diocesan Reading Union: 'It is true that everyone's time is always being broken in upon, but the people whom I have known who were able to get through most work are those who can make use, not only of six hours at a time, anyone can do that, but of six minutes at a time. It is by gaining the power of using odd minutes that the most valuable work in life can be done.'[7]

It was by filling every moment that Creighton was able to achieve so much. The fruit of these years at Embleton included several historical manuals in addition to the volumes on the Papacy. There were also numerous book reviews for the *Manchester Guardian* and a number of learned journals. He was sensitive about criticizing his friends and could never bring himself to write an ill-natured review, even when anonymity made candour less daring. With his hand on his heart and without smugness he was able to confess: 'I never wrote an ill-natured article about anybody in my life and I never review the book of anyone I know unless I am conscientiously prepared to praise it. I have sent many books back to editors saying that I know the writers, and think their books rubbish, and do not think I am the right man to say so.'

As select preacher and examiner in the History School, Creighton was able to maintain his ties with the University of Oxford during these busy years in his northern parish. Happy and industrious as his life was, he still had one eye on the University. His ambitions were scholarly and academic rather than ecclesiastical. The one occasion in his life when he took steps to promote his own interests was when Stubbs left the

Regius Professorship of Modern History at Oxford to become
Bishop of Chester. Creighton wrote to several influential
friends to express his desire for the vacant chair. His overtures
were unavailing, but it was not long before the creation of the
Dixie Professorship of Ecclesiastical History at Cambridge
opened up the way for his return to the university world.

Ambitions—even worthy and reasonable ones as Creighton's
were—often bring loss and gain in their fulfilment. When
Creighton was elected to the professorship in May 1884, he felt
the pain as well as the delight of his achievement. The very
ordinariness of parish life had meant much to him. The text for
the farewell sermon at Embleton was aptly chosen: 'Because I
have you in my heart.' Creighton was no sentimentalist. Most
people found him austere, but not stiff. He had little in common
with the quarry-men, farm labourers, and fisher-folk of his
scattered Northumbrian parish. And yet in spite of all the
difference of outlook and interest that separated parson and
people, there was a real bond between them and they both
knew it and loved it. The dedicated scholar could be happy with
his books—but not completely happy. The cultivated gentleman loved dining with the Greys at Falloden, but 'high'
society, even intellectual high society, was not everything.
The ballast which made the ship of his life sail smoothly was
provided by the humdrum routine, the comings and goings of
parish life. What made life lyrical rather than prosaic for the
Vicar of Embleton was the realization that there were really no
ordinary people, that the man in the street was a fiction. There
were only interesting individuals even if, at times, the most
interesting feature of their individuality was their tiresomeness.
Remote, grey, and bleak though the parish was, it could not be
dull for the pastor of the flock who believed in his job and
was uncommonly good at doing it.

His friend Mrs. T. H. Ward wrote to him: 'You have seen the
elemental human things nearer far than most men of letters have
a chance of seeing them, and now you will carry with you all this
fruitful experience to enrich the scholar's life that is to be.'

Before he left Embleton he visited every house in the parish

B

leaving a photograph of himself. There was no vanity in this gesture. The people were conscious that a man of rare distinction had occupied the Vicarage and they liked to think that they had some share in his fame. In terms of personal satisfaction the ten years at Embleton were unsurpassed and Creighton was not the first eminent ecclesiastic—and doubtless will not be the last—to write from the top of the tree: 'As I look back I see that the happiest time was that which I spent in a country parish.'

CAMBRIDGE AND WORCESTER

There is abundant evidence that Creighton was a stimulating teacher. Education, at all levels, was one of his lifelong interests. He began, as he once said, 'absolutely and entirely ignorant of the art of teaching; all I learnt about it was at the expense of those whom I taught'. If education was a choice between learning something about everything or everything about something, Creighton favoured the latter. He warned his pupils about the snare of little books. 'I never was able to read a small book on history; a compendium or handbook is an abomination to me.' He saw the value of intellectual study as a discipline for the moulding of character. 'There is no discipline so admirable as that of learning to weigh and balance evidence. To see how easy it is to be deceived, to strive conscientiously in our own case to distinguish between what is plausible and what is true, to choose the good and refuse the evil—these should be the results of methodical study.' The main duty of the teacher is to stimulate the curiosity and develop the observing power of the student. There is no end to the process, for the true student is never satisfied with the knowledge he has gained. 'Self-satisfaction is the death of the mind as truly as it is the death of the soul.' These were some of the principles enunciated by Creighton and exemplified by him in his life as scholar and teacher.

Creighton was the first Dixie Professor of Ecclesiastical History. Before his arrival in Cambridge church history had meant to most Cambridge men the study of the ancient

Church, a field in which Lightfoot had set the standard of distinguished scholarship. 'The electors were determined that the continuity of Christian history should not be overlooked.'[8] Creighton was a specialist in a later period and his appointment and teaching secured this study of the continuity of church life and institutions. In lectures and seminars as well as in long walks with his abler pupils his work as teacher was pursued. His six years at Cambridge were also fruitful in his own historical writing. The third and fourth volumes of the *History of the Papacy* appeared in 1887, and to this period belong his *Life of Cardinal Wolsey* and his *History of Carlisle*. He also helped to found the *English Historical Review* and was its first editor.

In the summer of 1885 Gladstone appointed Creighton to a Canonry at Worcester, and he was delighted to spend the vacations there and to have the opportunity, which he readily seized, of entering into the life of the Cathedral and the city. As Examining Chaplain to the Bishop (Philpot) he was able to promote some reforms in the ordination arrangements at Worcester. They were as perfunctory and unedifying as the arrangements for Creighton's own ordination at Oxford had been. He writes, 8 April 1886, '. . . the ordinations here simply fill me with despair. They are of the oldest fashion. The examination is held in Worcester immediately before ordination. The candidates live in hotels and see the Bishop for a moment on Saturday afternoon in the most formal way, and are ordained the next day without a word of counsel. . . . The whole thing is as unedifying as it could be.' Under gentle pressure from Creighton changes were made. The examination was held some weeks before the ordination; the candidates were lodged in houses in the College and met together for services and addresses. All this the Bishop accepted willingly, though he begged that he should not be asked to allow the men to be ordained in surplices instead of black gowns. So this point was not pressed, and black gowns continued to be the sartorial fashion at Bishop Philpot's ordinations.

The Worcester Canonry provided Creighton with opportunities to develop his powers as a preacher. His Cathedral sermons were almost entirely extempore. The only record of them is a few brief notes and jottings, not infrequently in pencil, on half-sheets of notepaper and backs of envelopes. They have a scrappy appearance and give little indication of the content and scarcely any indication of the quality of his discourses. In the homiletic art he was no model for lesser men. His immediate preparation was often short, sometimes non-existent, but he was able to draw readily and swiftly upon his well-stored mind and he had the gift of lucidity. He had no histrionic tricks; he never sought to be a popular preacher or to tickle the fancy of his hearers. He scorned extraneous aids by which poor matter may be made to pass muster for oratory. 'We are severe critics', he says, 'of one another; it is the function of the preacher to induce us to turn the power of criticism upon ourselves.'

He avoided controversial questions and subjects of Biblical and theological criticism and debate, and later advised his clergy to avoid these themes. In this he underestimated the interest of people in controversial topics and their hunger for explanation and help on matters that were under dispute. His intention, however, was right, namely that preaching should be constructive and affirmative. Years later he enlarged on his purpose in preaching in an address to his own clergy.

I would dissuade my clergy from controversial sermons. The ordinary services of the Church are not the place for apologetics. Men come to church that they may be built up in the faith, that they may have God and His law, Christ and His redemption, brought nearer to their souls by the Holy Spirit. Strength comes to them through the simple and straightforward utterances of a soul which is at peace with God, through the manifestation of a personality which they have seen active during the week, coming in and going out among them, living in sympathy with the lives of others, striving to remove temptations, to console and uplift. They do not wish for discussions, however clever, on the questions of the day. These are ever with them—in the newspaper, in business, in talk. These are best treated in free discussion;

for they present themselves differently to every man, and do not admit of general answers. But all men long for a firmer hold on great principles, for the assurance of spiritual power, for warnings against temptation, for some spur to greater effort, for a higher and nobler view of life, its duties and its possibilities. If you give them this they will thank you.[9]

No doubt adherence to his own principles made Creighton's preaching unexciting. He was so scrupulously fair by nature, so moderate by temperament that he was incapable of a harangue. Denunciation was not his line and he suspected the prophet. A letter he wrote at this time, though not concerned with preaching, affords a clue to the understanding of his approach to the pulpit.

I think that one of the nuisances of the present day is the attempted revival of the prophet. Carlyle, Froude, Ruskin, all bore me in their prophetic capacity. It is a cheap line to denounce, it satisfies the sense that something ought to be done. I am weary of denunciation. We of this world all go about the world abusing everybody else, and each forgetting to amend himself. . . . I respect Ruskin's goodness but his method is disastrous. The times do not want an historical prophet denouncing woe; they want the spirit of loving sympathy. How large-hearted was Jesus, how soberminded, how 'sweetly reasonable' as Matthew Arnold puts it. Teacher for teacher there is more in Matthew Arnold than in Ruskin. Both are one-sided, both omit much, but the spirit, the tone of Matthew Arnold is fruitful while that of Ruskin, save in art, is not.[10]

Creighton's published sermons are plain and straightforward. They are full of moral earnestness combined with an extraordinary sanity. Professor Owen Chadwick has drawn attention to the change in Creighton's preaching as the years passed. The earlier sermons are practical and ethical, the earlier they are the more moralistic. One of the few sermons he is recorded as having preached in Emmanuel College Chapel was devoted to a criticism of the undergraduates for wasting their afternoon

in watching football matches. When he became a bishop he had
to search for the theological principles which were necessary for
a solution of the practical and pastoral questions which faced
him. The episcopal sermons, though still practical, ethical, and
the fruit of experience of life, are more theological in their
foundations. He was not everyman's preacher but some, and
those not the least discerning, preferred him to any other.
Creighton the preacher is well summed up in an appreciative
comment by a fellow historian, Charles Bigg:

> As a speaker he was amazingly ready; all his knowledge, all
> his powers were instantaneously at command. He did not
> care for eloquence, indeed he despised it; what he aimed at
> was instruction, and for this he always looked more to
> principles than to facts. He was not moving or pathetic,
> but stimulating and persuasive. His voice filled the largest
> building without an effort and yet did not raise an echo.
> People, especially men, flocked to hear him both at Worcester
> and Peterborough. He was never rhetorical or sensational,
> but you carried away the impression of a man who had given
> not his heart only, but a fine intelligence, to the cause which
> he preached.[11]

BISHOP OF PETERBOROUGH

Although well established in the academic world, Creighton
was a stranger to the world of church affairs and had little
contact with church dignitaries. With the exception of Bishop
Stubbs, with whom his relations were literary rather than
ecclesiastical, his episcopal contacts were confined to his own
diocesans at Durham, Newcastle, and Worcester. He had never
sat in Convocation nor sought any place on those central
church committees in London where the aspirants to high
ecclesiastical office are to be found. It is, therefore, doubtful
whether Creighton would have been elevated to the bench if the
appointment of bishops had been in the hands of the Church.
In December 1890 he was offered a Canonry at Windsor, but
before he had been installed a letter came from Lord Salisbury

saying he had the Queen's permission to nominate him to the diocese of Peterborough. Creighton had not sought it and did not want it. He wrote to one of his friends: 'A bishopric is to me after the flesh a terrible nuisance. But how is a man to refuse the responsibilities of his branch of the service? I saw no way out. I am an object of compassion; but I must not grumble, for that is foolish. Only, as hundreds of men are pining for such a post, and I am not, it seems mere contrareity.' The appointment was 'a terrible nuisance' because he realized that the days of his scholarly activity were numbered. To another friend he writes: 'My peace of mind is gone; my books will be shut up; my mind will go to seed; I shall utter nothing but platitudes for the rest of my life, and everybody will write letters in the newspapers about my iniquities.'

He wrote, perhaps, more truly than he knew. But for the moment he need have had no such fears. The Peterborough years were the calm before the storm. He was little troubled with ritual problems in the 676 parishes of the diocese. His own wide sympathies, his liberal views and religious tolerance enabled him to win the respect and loyalty of the clergy and laity. The same qualities secured for him the respect and goodwill of the large nonconformist element in Northampton and Leicester. A bitter and long-drawn-out strike in the boot-trade troubled him greatly and in working for its solution he reveals his ability as statesman and administrator in his grasp of both general principles and intricate details.

In May 1896 he represented the Church of England at the Coronation of the Emperor Nicholas II in Moscow. Archbishop Benson sent him off with 'the smartest clothes the law allows'. Creighton's own cope was considered unsuitable so he borrowed one of the Westminster coronation robes of crimson velvet and gold, and with his own mitre and crozier, he clearly enjoyed his part in the dazzling spectacle. Lytton Strachey seized on this exciting moment in Creighton's life:

... he tasted to the full the splendour of the great ceremonies and the extraordinary display of autocratic power. That there might have been some degree of spiritual squalor mixed with these magnificent appearances never seemed to occur to him. He was fascinated by the apparatus of a mighty organisation and with unerring instinct made straight for the prime mover of it, the chief Procurator of the Holy Synod, the sinister Pobiedonostzeff, with whom he struck up a warm friendship. He was presented to the Emperor and Empress, and found them charming. 'I was treated with great distinction, as I was called in first. The Empress looked very nice, dressed in white silk.' The aristocratic Acton would, no doubt, have viewed things in a different light. Absolute power corrupts absolutely —so he had said; but Creighton had forgotten the remark. He was no Daniel. He saw no writing on the wall.[12]

Certainly Creighton was deeply impressed by this experience, but he knew too much from his study of European politics of the frailties and self-seeking motives of men in power to be so naïve and blind as Strachey's sardonic comment would suggest.

The busy but comparatively peaceful years as Bishop of Peterborough did not altogether preclude further literary labours. The fifth and final volume of his *History of the Papacy* appeared, and his book on Queen Elizabeth. In 1893-4 he delivered the Hulsean Lectures on *Persecution and Tolerance*, a 'trifling contribution to a great subject', as he called it. Trifling though his treatment may be, it was a subject for which he was well suited by both his own studies and his own temperament. His description of the tolerant man is almost a self-portrait.

The tolerant man has decided opinions, but recognises the process by which he reached them, and keeps before himself the truth that they can only be profitably spread by repeating in the case of others a similar process to that through which he passed himself. He always keeps in view the hope of spreading his own opinions, but he endeavours to do so by producing conviction. He is virtuous, not because he puts his own opinions out of sight, nor because he thinks that other opinions are as good as his own, but because his opinions are so real to him that he would not have anyone else hold them with less reality.[13]

Tolerance is needful to the individual; for it is the expression of that reverence for others which forms a great part of the lesson which Christ came to teach him. It is the means whereby he learns to curb self-conceit, and submit to the penetrating discipline imposed by Christian love.[14]

Creighton's own life was soon to be beset by the vagaries of intolerant self-regarding men, and his happiness and his health were soon to be impaired by their wilful and inconsiderate ways. The concluding words of his Hulsean Lectures reveal the spirit in which he faced the problems that were soon to confront him in London: 'There is always a temptation to the possessors of power—be they an individual, an institution or a class—to use it selfishly or harshly. Liberty is a tender plant and needs jealous watching. It is always unsafe in the world, and is only secure under the guardianship of the Church; for the Church possesses the knowledge of man's eternal destiny—which alone can justify his claim to freedom.'[15] Creighton knew, better than most, that liberty, far from being secured, had often been destroyed by the Church, but that there was no other final security for it than that supplied by the Christian doctrine of man's spiritual nature as a child of God and as one who was made in the divine image.

BISHOP OF LONDON

'Next to the Bishopric of Rome the Bishopric of London is the most important position in Christendom.' The remark is attributed to Dean Stanley and Creighton recalled it when he was appointed to the diocese of London. Gossip writers who, then as now, enjoyed idle speculations about the higher ecclesiastical appointments had mentioned Creighton's name as the likely successor to Benson at Canterbury. He neither desired nor expected to succeed to Augustine's Chair, and when Benson died Temple went to Canterbury and Creighton became Bishop of London, complaining that it was 'a nuisance going to new work' and 'a bore becoming a more important person'.

Kensit, the leading trouble-maker in the Protestant underworld, was on his tracks from the start. He made one of his customary disturbances when Creighton's election as Bishop of London was confirmed in the Church of St. Mary le Bow. Kensit objected to the appointment on the grounds that Creighton had worn a mitre, and had promoted unsuitable persons. The objection was overruled and as they left the church Creighton shook hands with Kensit, saying he was sure they would understand one another as they became better acquainted. As a sentiment it was a courteous gesture; as a prophecy it was wide of the mark. The troubles which were to darken and shorten his days had begun.

Creighton disliked complicated administrative machinery, but some changes in the organization and routine of his life were now necessary. At Peterborough a clerk in the Diocesan Registry had helped him for an hour or two each day. Now he had to engage a Domestic Chaplain. He employed no other secretarial help and had a hearty dislike of shorthand secretaries. Occasionally he would dictate letters to his daughters. For the most part he answered letters himself, writing with great rapidity and in any odd moment of time, not excluding the time he spent attending meetings of the Ecclesiastical Commission or of the Trustees of the British Museum. Letters poured from his pen, letters of business, domestic letters to sons and daughters, to nephews and nieces, private letters of spiritual counsel and advice to correspondents known and unknown who sought his help, and never in vain. His many letters of consolation, sympathy, and encouragement are all refreshingly free from sentimentality. He was at his best in writing to those in trouble and perplexity. The following is a typical extract from such a letter. It is to a man unknown to Creighton who had written to say he was dying of a painful and incurable disease and that he could not accept the Christian faith. He had implored Creighton to tell him what book he should study to guide and help him.

. . . Religion must be a matter of belief, not of proof. It depends on a consciousness of the relation between our soul and God. Immortality depends on the knowledge of the meaning of our soul's life which we obtain from looking at it in the light of God. The more we find our soul, the more readily do we see God in the person of Jesus Christ. Look back upon your own life, your growth, the times of providence, the presence of God's love. Do you think that this wonderful process can come to an abrupt end?

These are general considerations. I can only commend them to you. There is nothing that can be said in proof of this to you. Look into your own heart; pray, and ask God to enlighten you. Reading will not help you: argument on either side is barren. The only thing I can recommend to you is the Gospel of St. John. Read it and weigh it. Consider the view of life which it contains. May God bless you, for He alone can do so.[16]

The marvel is that Creighton was able to find time to write so many personal letters in spite of the pressure of his life in London. In the first year he delivered 294 sermons and addresses. In June of that year (1897) he writes: 'I shall soon cease to have any intellect at all. I never have time to read a serious book or take in new ideas.' In August: 'I have the melancholy feeling that I am now quite played out. I must go on as I am till I fizzle away.' And again a few months later: 'I am perpetually overwhelmed with work. I have to express more opinions than I have time to verify.'

So much of the work was impersonal and this made it the harder to bear. 'It requires all my efforts to remain human in this inhuman spot, with all the business I have to do—business which is done in a rush and which depends solely on judgement, and rarely calls for any personal touch. The only things that cheer me are the letters that I get from folk in my diocese submitting their difficulties, small and personal: sometimes a young man's trouble how to be honest in business; a soldier's

love story and its difficulties: such things I get and they bring
me back to human life.'

He had too strong a sense of duty to indulge in self-pity and,
being as much a man of affairs as a scholar, he was following his
natural bent in being closely associated with the life of the
nation in its capital city. There is no boasting in the summary
he gives to one correspondent of a day's activity:

> Would you like a record of my doings yesterday? I wrote
> letters till 11.10. Then I had a Confirmation at 11.30. At 1.0
> I went on a deputation to the Home Secretary and addressed
> him about Sunday Newspapers. Then I hastened to lunch
> with the American Ambassador, where I sat between the
> Marquis of Lansdowne and Mr. Goschen. Then I went to a
> meeting of Waifs and Strays where I was in the Chair. Then
> to a meeting of the London University Commission which
> lasted till 6.30. Then I went to dinner with Mr. Asquith,
> and met the Duke of Devonshire and Mr. Balfour. That was
> pretty violent.[17]

'It is difficult', he once said in an after-dinner speech, 'to
analyse the characteristics of the sub-species "prelates", whose
habitats are sporadic, and of many of whom the habitats are
the last places in which one is likely to find them.' Notwith-
standing the hectic life he had to lead he filled it with distinction
and could have borne it gladly if it had not been for the ritual
troubles and the buffets and assaults he received from extremists at both ends of the ecclesiastical spectrum. He found the
London diocese in great chaos. Temple had worked hard
himself and let everyone else work in the way they liked.
London was full of free-lances, eccentrics, and individualists.
There was little sense of the unity of the Church. Church life in
London was a vast urban sea of isolationism. When neighbours
were nearest to each other they were most distant and cut off
from each other. Each man lived in a little world of his own
(his parish) within the larger characterless world of London
(the diocese). Indeed the diocese had little or no meaning. 'The
difficulties of the clergy in this diocese are enormous: isolation,

congregationalism, little intercourse with one another or the Bishop, little sense of the largeness of the Church as a whole or of the end of its working.'

Creighton tackled the ritual disorders in the diocese chiefly in private conference and by gentle persuasion. Thus he laboured to bring the diverse strands of church life in London into unity and harmony. A few days after his enthronement he wrote to the Rev. E. G. Hodge:

> You are the only one of my parochial clergy whom I really know, and you know something at least of the spirit in which I try to do the difficult work of a Bishop in the Church of England as it is this day. Those difficulties are at their height in London, and you know that I have no belief in my exclusive possession of wisdom. But you also know that my sympathies are genuinely with every form of opinion, and that my object is to bring them all into close union, without asking them to compromise, but only to be large hearted. Differences do not matter, but the way in which we express them.[18]

It is probable that Creighton was expected to be more in sympathy with the Anglo-Catholics than proved to be the case. After all, he was a high churchman and had gone to the Moscow Coronation in 'the best clothes the law allows'. But he was also a patriot and a nationalist, some would say too insular in his outlook. He so greatly revered the Church of England that he could not look favourably on any teaching or ritual and ceremonial practices that seemed to him disloyal to the English Church and a disavowal of the Anglican position.

In addition to many patient and private interviews Creighton sought to achieve unity and harmony in the diocese by enlarging, as opportunity occurred, on the principles of the Church of England. Many addresses and charges were devoted to this theme. In them he expresses his view of the English Church, neither a medieval church nor a church of the continental reformed type, but a church with a unique position resting on an appeal to sound learning. The English reformers appealed to Scripture and history. Undisturbed by the influences which distorted the reformation movement elsewhere, they were able to strip off medieval accretions of doctrine and ceremony in an attempt to restore a more primitive simplicity based on the Bible and the early Fathers. No doubt this is an over-simplified picture of the sixteenth-century Reformation, and no doubt Creighton, as he once described himself, was a fanatical Anglican, but there was nothing narrow and rigid in the position he adopted. He could not approve of doctrines being taught which indicated a return to Romanism or Medievalism or which amounted to a definite departure from the distinctive position of the Church of England. On the other hand, he was ready to allow a wide latitude. He believed in comprehension rather than uniformity and, as he admitted, he had almost a craze for liberty. He was essentially a peacemaker who longed for peace and quiet. The tragedy of his official life is that in his later years he enjoyed so little of either. Many of his clergy accepted his rulings loyally, but there were sufficient recalcitrants to hound him to death. The extremists on both sides gave him no rest. There were times when a mixture of asperity and irritability, combined with a playfulness that was always breaking through, prompted him to a remark that was more telling than discreet, as when he told one high churchman: 'The Catholic Church must go into the waste-paper-basket.' Or again, when a deputation of clergy who were defending their use of incense turned to Creighton and said: 'But my Lord, we have a cure of souls.' 'Yes,' retorted the Bishop, 'and you think souls like herrings can't be cured without smoke.' Not all his witticisms were so barbed. At a school prize-giving at Highgate he said: 'The days have long ceased when a bishop could visit Highgate woods for the purpose of hunting. I presume they used to go there to hunt boars; nowadays bores hunt me, even in my own house.'

The steps taken by Creighton to deal with the ritual troubles will be described in a later chapter. The end of his life was clouded by them, but the Boer War was another source of sorrow. Though a strong nationalist, a fervent patriot, and an admirer of the English and all things English, Creighton saw in the Boer War a rebuke to British pride and self-conceit. The lesson of humility was the lesson the British public had to learn. Meanwhile, the war brought some relief to hard-pressed ecclesiastics. 'The Public Mind', he said, 'will pitch into the Boers instead of the Bishops.' Creighton deplored the petty squabbles within the Church that had sapped its spiritual vigour and left it unable to teach the nation the lesson that was necessary at this time. 'I wish I could say the Church had been doing its best to teach this needful lesson to the English people. Unfortunately, it has only been reproducing in its own quarrels the temper that prevails. Just in the point where an example was most needed it has not been given. The Church has adopted the method of politics. It has presented the appearance of parties contending against one another. It has injured its spiritual influence by descending to trivial disputes. It has not shown the English people a higher spirit or a better way.'[19]

This was more disastrous in a national Church than in a sectarian body. Creighton's reverence for the Church of England, at times, no doubt, an excessive reverence, stemmed from its close identity with the life of the nation. 'I am an enthusiastic and fanatical Anglican.' The English Church was the nation in its spiritual aspect. The internal wranglings of the Church sapped its life-blood and prevented it from fulfilling its unique mission. As his life ebbed away, and he was incapacitated by ulceration of the stomach due to strain and worry, he strove to pull the Church together and make it conscious of its true character and purpose. As the years went by he had appreciated increasingly that his mission in life was to try to get people to understand the meaning of the Church of England. He bent all his great powers of mind and heart to that end. He lived in its service and died its victim. Years before, in the serene Cambridge days, he had written to a close friend: 'I should wish for my own part to pass away while I was still active, and to leave to others a memory of myself at my best, before bodily frailty had dimmed my mind or wasted my faculties.' His wish was granted. He died on 14 January 1901, and was buried in the crypt of St. Paul's.

2 · THE INNER MAN

WHAT manner of man was he? In appearance tall and dignified, with aquiline face, bald forehead, a full reddish beard, and gold-rimmed spectacles which he never removed except in bed. He was not demonstrative but rather restrained and he used little gesture in speaking. Had he been less striking and imposing he might have been thought a dapper man, for he was always careful of his dress and appearance. At times he gave to those who did not know him well the impression of being cynical, partly because, being undemonstrative, he did not wear his heart on his sleeve, partly because he used often to conceal his true feelings and hide himself in playful paradox. There was no pomposity in his dignity and in all his official dealings he showed great patience. In public he never allowed himself to be irritated, brusque, or grumpy, though he could be stern, even severe, 'beneficially severe', as one of his friends described him. Dr. Bigg, another church historian, who knew him well, records: 'Once or twice I have heard him speak very sternly, but I never saw him ruffled, embarrassed or peevish.'[1]

He could show another face at home among his large family of three sons and four daughters. Mrs. Creighton writes: 'Like all men of highly-strung natures he had a somewhat impatient and irritable temper. This was, as a rule, absolutely under control. I do not think he ever showed temper or irritability at meetings or with his pupils, or on any public occasions. But in private life he would sometimes express displeasure or vexation in sharp and cutting words; those who were nearest and dearest to him alone seemed able to arouse his irritation.'[2]

In politics he was a liberal, though he was dubious about the wisdom of clergymen taking an active role in party politics. His own conduct was somewhat equivocal in this respect. In the General Election of 1880 he spoke at several meetings on behalf of the Liberal candidate for South Northumberland, but was careful not to take part in the election in his own neighbourhood at Embleton, except to lend his pony carriage to take voters to the poll. In later life, as his own responsibilities increased and the Liberal Party split over Home Rule, Creighton became less of a party man. This waning of his allegiance to a party suited his temperament, for he was one who questioned the salvability of politicians.

Even in the Embleton days he foresaw the inevitability of the trend towards Socialism: 'I do not mean that the cut and dried system of Socialism will be accepted by the State in the lifetime of any one of us; but I do think that legislation will more and more assume a socialistic bias and rightly so, and that the rights of the individual will be less and less regarded when they evidently clash with the welfare of the people as a whole.'[3] But he saw also the inherent danger of the system, and years later he writes: 'Socialism can only rest on a vigorous system of discipline, which can only be tyranny if it is not accepted on moral grounds from within. Yet the socialists dare not say so; they dare not even hint at the necessity of discipline. Everything is pursued and recommended on the grounds that liberty means doing what one likes.'[4]

It is a measure of Creighton's discernment and breadth of interest that although he was in some ways so characteristic of the best of Victorian high-mindedness, he was greatly attracted to Samuel Butler, who rebelled against it. Butler frequently visited Creighton, who was impressed by Butler's writing. Creighton had taken the initiative in arranging the first of their many meetings. 'The first time', writes Samuel Butler, 'that Dr. Creighton asked me to come down to Peterborough, in 1894, before he became Bishop of London, I was a little doubtful whether to go or not. As usual I consulted my good clerk, Alfred, who said, "Let me have a look at his letter, Sir." I gave him the letter, and he said: "I see, Sir, there is a crumb of tobacco in it; I think you may go." I went and enjoyed myself very much. I should like to add that there are very few men who have impressed me so profoundly and so

favourably as Dr. Creighton.'[5] Mrs. Grosvenor (a friend of
Samuel Butler) adds an interesting footnote to this first meeting
between Butler and Creighton: 'He [Butler] asked me if I
would lend him a Prayer Book as he thought the Bishop's
man ought to find one in his portmanteau when he unpacked,
the visit being from a Saturday to Monday. I fetched one and
as I handed it to him he said: "Is it cut?".'[6] Thereafter Butler
was a frequent visitor and the two men, so different in so many
ways, were greatly attracted to each other.

No doubt Butler the independent-minded, bubble-pricking
rebel appealed to Creighton's sense of fun and to his distaste for
humbug. In spite of all his moral earnestness and his elevation
of duty, he could often give the impression of flippancy, even of
cynicism. 'No people do so much harm as those who go about
doing good' was one of his sayings. He could not endure a man
who calls the Church 'She'. Priggishness was anathema to him
and he was always quick and ready to deflate the cocksure.
'What books would you recommend for devotional reading?'
asks a prim little man. 'I do not know what devotional reading
is,' was the Bishop's reply. So he often puzzled people, for he was
a man who usually hid himself in playfulness and paradox.
Dr. Bigg sums him up thus: 'The foundation of his character
was given him by the North Country and was very grave and
sedate.'[7] So, too, he was severe and stern—stern with himself
and with those for whom he felt any responsibility. But there
was another side—the sparkling and the humorous side, so that
the gravity was matched by light-heartedness as the severity
was matched by sympathy. He was both grave and gay.

Creighton's religion was Christo-centric. 'Christianity meant
not a system, not the Church, but a person—Jesus.' This is the
heart and centre of his own religious faith and experience. The
same central thought occurs over and over again in intimate
personal letters, in addresses and Confirmation talks. 'Personal
trust in a person, this is the secret of true religion. Outward
things, systems, doctrines, are only useful as they keep open the
way to Jesus, and point to Him as the object of the soul's
desire.'[8] Without religion there could be no understanding,

nor could there be any understanding without faith and feeling.

> If we try to grasp the world as it is, language fails us in our attempts to *explain*—we must *feel*, we must *sympathize*, we must break out into parable. Life can only be explained by a Life: and I see in Jesus that life of which all other life is but a partial reflex. I always find that scepticism narrows the real problem, refuses to face the actual facts, substitutes energy in reforming the world for power to deal with it as it is. I can sympathize with all that it has to say and all that it tries to do; but there is so much beyond. . . . Try to explain yourself as you can, there is a vast residuum that you cannot turn into shape. How is all this to be dealt with? I answer only by conscious communion with a Person who is Life and Truth.[9]

These words were written in a private letter, but they are echoed in many of his more formal and public utterances. Thus when preaching before the British Association at Ipswich in 1895 on the processes by which knowledge is gained he leads up to the same conclusion: 'The pursuit of knowledge teaches reverence and humility; it requires for its success seriousness, sobriety, a sense of limitation, above all a sense of relationship to universal truth.'[10] To Creighton no grasp of knowledge was possible without a conception of the unity of truth. All knowledge becomes coherent 'by the revelation of God contained in scripture. That revelation is, like all others, progressive, for it is the revelation of a Person, the Lord Jesus Christ, and that Person is the centre of all other revelations, the point to which they run.'[11] This was the central belief of his life and the focus of his faith.

Creighton's religion was experiential, ethical, and practical. This made him effective in addressing children. On one occasion he tells the story of a child who wrote an essay on a cat. 'The cat is said to have nine lives, but in this country it seldom needs them all because of Christianity.' 'This sentence', he went on to say, 'had a good deal packed away in it . . . the

child knew that general kindness and love was the first principle of Christianity . . . it is this that you too ought to have, a
sense of what it is that Christianity really does.'[12]

Creighton's mind was historical rather than speculative.
There are no indications that he ever had any intellectual
doubts and difficulties. He was not troubled about miracles.
'The gospel is the truth to which nothing can be added and
from which nothing can be taken away. The more we consider
it, the more we shall see that the gospel is the greatest and most
practical message of the eternal truth of all times both ancient
and modern, of that truth which alone enables a man to steer
his way through the world.'[13] His faith was simple, but never
obscurantist. He accepted Biblical criticism and assured results
of scholarship but he had no patience with, or time for, the
more startling and popular expressions of it. To a young friend
he writes:

> I have never yet answered your question about Renan's
> *Vie de Jésus*, because I did not know what to say. I never read
> it myself, so I don't know anything about it. I am opposed to
> protection as you know; but on the other hand I am opposed
> to reading a book because it is naughty or unorthodox. Read
> it if you have any reason to believe it contains anything you
> want to know, but don't ever read a book because it made a
> sensation and obtained a notoriety by being naughty or
> unorthodox. I don't know that Renan's *Vie de Jésus* has
> anything to add to one's conception of Christ; I don't at all
> like that style of book: the Gospels are the best life of Christ,
> and historically the only authentic ones, and all such lives
> as Renan's are merely sensational ways of putting popularly
> results of criticism, which persons had much better take as
> results of criticism, not in the shape of a sentimental novel.[14]

In matters of belief he was clear about the essentials while
recognizing the limitation set upon our understanding. 'The
fact of the existence of religion provokes scepticism because if
there was a god who could be entirely known he would then
cease to be the God who helps us. . . ."Verily thou art a God

that hidest thyself." '[15] But though he was little troubled by the intellectual difficulties of religion, he knew and recognized the difficulty of prayer. In a letter to a niece he says: 'Yes, it is a very extraordinary thing how hard a thing it is to say one's prayers rightly. Everybody always feels it. . . . I always think the Collect is so wise which claims for us no more than to be "those to whom Thou hast given an hearty desire to pray". It does not say that we can pray, but that God has given us a wish to pray. . . . I believe that everybody supposes that everybody else prays more easily than they do, but it is difficult for us all.'[16]

Creighton was essentially an optimist about human nature. Good and evil were curiously mixed, but there was more good than evil, and evil was 'always tending to be wiped out if it did not improve'. He was always making allowances for others and he followed his own counsel. 'It is better to think people better than they are than worse than they are; one can only hope that experience will teach them.'[17]

Experience had taught him and yet in one sense he changed little. The boy who had written the long Pastoral to teach the school monitors their duty was essentially the same person as the historian who was fascinated not by art or imagination, but by conscience, and was the same person as the high-minded prelate who strove to make the Church of England conscious of its divine mission and purpose in the life of the nation. And this same person was a boy, a pastor, and a prelate all in one. The prelate without the boy would have been insufferable; the dignified and distinguished official would have been formidable beyond endurance but for the twinkle and light-heartedness of the boy and the zeal and love of the pastor.

3 · THE HISTORIAN

CREIGHTON was one of the founders and was the first editor of the *English Historical Review*. In the prefatory note to the first volume he explains his view of history and his editorial policy: 'The object of history is to discover and set forth facts, and he who confines himself to this object, forbearing acrimonious language, can usually escape the risk of giving offence. . . . Recognizing the value of the light which history may shed on practical problems, we shall not hesitate to let that light be reflected in our pages, whenever we can be sure that it is daylight, free from any tinge of partisanship.' It was a characteristic utterance and it found complete fulfilment in his own historical work. He forbore from acrimonious language; the offence he gave was for not giving offence; the light that shines from his pages is certainly a grey light and no historian was ever more free from any tinge of partisanship. 'The biscuit', as Lytton Strachey said, 'is certainly exceedingly dry, but at any rate there are no weevils in it.'[1] Ranke was his model. Acton had spoken of Ranke's 'merciful abstinence from strong language, his reserve in passing sentence'. The same is true of all Creighton's own work though, as we shall see, it was on these very counts that Acton criticized it.

As a historian Creighton's reputation rests upon his five-volume *History of the Papacy from the Great Schism to the Sack of Rome*. Throughout its intricate story Creighton exhibits what Acton called 'his sovereign impartiality'. It is indeed a remarkable achievement. His mastery of the tangled web of European politics, his scrupulous fairness and detachment, his terse and penetrating character sketches, his knowledge and understanding of the artistic movements of the period, his complete freedom from prejudice or partisanship, his refusal to condemn outright—all these features of his work make the book a plain unvarnished picture of the times. It is, however, a picture painted in depth. There are no moral lectures or purple passages, but there is the most lucid exposition of complicated political transactions and the intricate movements of thought in which they were set. It is in this kind of historical writing that Creighton excelled. In his view the writing of history was more akin to science than to novel writing, and there was no distinction to be drawn between church history and secular history.

In his inaugural lecture at Cambridge he had put his cards on the table. 'Ecclesiastical history must be pursued in exactly the same way, and with exactly the same spirit as any other branch of history. The aim of the investigation is simply the discovery of truth.'[2] Colourful opinions often rest on frail foundations of fact. 'When we stand aside and watch for a moment it is almost painful to observe on what scanty fund of real knowledge the strongest and most decided opinions are accepted and upheld.'[3]

If there are any lessons to be drawn from history it is not the historian's business to point to them. Let the events speak for themselves. 'My view of history is not to approach things with any preconceived ideas, but with the natural *pietas* and sympathy which I try to feel towards all men who do, or try to do great things. *Mentem mortalia tangunt* is my motto. I try to put myself in their place: to see their limitations and leave the course of events to pronounce the verdict upon systems and men alike.'[4]

Believing, as he did, that the good are not so good as they think they are and the bad are not so bad as others think them, Creighton's judgements are never black or white. Seeing both sides of every penny, he never came down on any side. 'It is an education in itself to realize how much is to be said on both sides in politics, whether those of our own day or a former time.'[5] There is, of course, another and very different approach to history in which the historian is expected to get inside the situation and make up his own mind and try to carry his readers with him. Creighton was not of that school. 'When you begin to draw definite lessons and morals from history, you at once cease to be searching after truth, because you have a bias which tends to take you to one side or another.'[6] He was, perhaps, not so free from a point of view as he thought. In the opinion of Dr. Claude Jenkins, 'he had prepossessions . . . even it may be prejudices of which he was only partly aware, but his mind was too sceptical, his learning too widely based, to make him the historian who became the idol of a party'.[7]

Such prepossessions as he had were unconscious. He went to history for facts and certainly had no thought of writing history to support any theories or opinions he might himself hold. He would not let himself go or give vent to his spleen.

> If I let go my grip on the general aspect of things in Europe and descend to personalities I am lost. I try to sympathize with everybody and see what was the subject of his activity. You can be very funny about modern politics if you resolve them into modes of Bismarck's digestion or Gladstone's success in felling trees, but these are backstairs politics and do not do much good. . . . Even now when I have Savonarola before me, I have to take his halo off and look at him as an ally of France and a disturber of Italian politics. . . . So, too, with the rest of them, Alexander VI was an unscrupulous politician, but not a villain, and Cesare Borgia was neither better nor worse than most other folk. All this is very dull to have to record. I would gladly denounce the abominations if I found them there. At present all that can be said of me is that I left a dull period of history as dull as I found it.[8]

Dullness was certainly one of the charges brought against Creighton's work and Creighton himself did not quarrel with this imputation. His most formidable critic, however, the Roman Catholic Lord Acton, complained on another score. Acton believed that great men are almost always bad men. It was the absence of a definite conclusion and Creighton's reluctance to condemn when condemnation was called for that moved Acton to write forcibly in criticism of Creighton's work. Reviewing the third and fourth volumes of the *History of the Papacy* he says Creighton 'is not striving to prove a case, or burrowing towards a conclusion, but wishes to pass through scenes of raging controversy and passion with a serene curiosity, a suspended judgement, a divided jury, and a pair of white gloves. Avoiding both alternatives of the prophet's mission, he will neither bless nor curse, and seldom invites his readers to execrate or to admire.'[9] Creighton was a little vexed at such strictures from so weighty a source. When the first two volumes appeared he had asked the publishers to arrange for them to be reviewed by Acton as the only man in England with sufficient learning to pass judgement on them. When the third and fourth volumes were published Creighton himself invited Acton to review them for the *English Historical Review*. 'I asked Lord Acton to review my Popes and he graciously consented. Now he sends me a review which reads to me like the utterance of a man who is in a furious passion but is incapable of clear expression.'[10] It was in correspondence with Creighton on the subject of this review that Acton enunciated his oft-quoted principle: 'Power tends to corrupt and absolute power corrupts absolutely.'[11] In this correspondence with Acton Creighton develops his approach to history:

> I remember that in 1880 I met John Bright at dinner: he was very cross, apparently a Cabinet Meeting had disagreed with him. Among the things he said was 'If the people knew what sort of men statesmen were, they would rise and hang the whole of them'. Next day I met a young man who had been talking to Gladstone who urged him to Parliamentary life saying, 'Statesmanship is the noblest way to serve mankind.' I am sufficient of a Hegelian to be able to combine both judgements; but the results of my combination cannot be expressed in the terms of the logic of Aristotle. In studying history the question of the salvability of an Archdeacon becomes indefinitely extended to all officials, kings and popes included. What I meant in my offending sentence in my preface was, that anyone engaged in great affairs occupied a representative position which required special consideration. Selfishness, even wrong-doing for an idea, an institution, the maintenance of an accepted view of the

basis of society, does not cease to be wrong-doing; but it is not quite the same as personal wrong-doing: it is more difficult to prove, and it does not equally shock the moral sense of others, or destroy the moral sense of the doer. The acts of men in power are determined by the effective force behind them of which they are the exponents: their morality is almost always lower than the morality of the mass of men; but there is generally a point fixed below which they cannot sink with impunity.[12]

The final volume of his *History of the Papacy from the Great Schism to the Sack of Rome* covers the opening phase in Luther's career. It is generally recognized that his treatment of Luther is a failure. Certainly it was the least satisfactory part of the whole work, though the competent treatment of so many miscellaneous minor figures provides some compensation. There are other compensations, too. Creighton's mastery of intricate detail is sustained to the end of the work. There is the same lucidity as distinguished the earlier volumes. But the character of Luther did not appeal to him; he was more drawn to the Italians than to the Germans; he was by nature an aesthete and he came to Italian history through Italian art. In the Reformation explosion Erasmus was the man after his own heart, but Erasmus steered clear of the blast as Creighton no doubt would have steered clear, too.

It is part of the paradox of Creighton that as a man of affairs he was high-minded, full of moral earnestness and a sense of duty, looking for principles as the basis of judgements and actions, whereas in the role of historian he was always on his guard against drawing moral lessons.

We like in reading Church history to seek for moral and religious edification and to find men whom we can admire. It is good to admire when we can; but it is bad to turn a man out of his actual shape that we may be better able to admire him. It is one of the great lessons that history can teach that there are few men, marvellously few, who retained purity of intention through their public career. We have to go aside from the beaten paths of affairs to find heroes, and the conflicts of the sixteenth century did not tend to develop those qualities which are most attractive to the Christian soul.[13]

He was, therefore, no hero-worshipper, though he shared the universal admiration for St. Francis. 'One man raises human nature to a level which it has never reached before. Then follow people who wear his clothes, and so you get hypocrisy.'[14]

There were some historical topics on which his sovereign impartiality served him well. His work on Cardinal Wolsey is a case in point. Whereas most men are judged by their achievements, Creighton perceived that Wolsey was greater than his achievements. He admired Wolsey's intellectual powers and force of character; he was more, much more, than an opportunist. In Creighton's judgement Wolsey was one of the greatest political geniuses that England ever produced, a man to be estimated by what he chose to do rather than by what he did. Equally successful was Creighton's study of Queen Elizabeth. He had lectured on the subject at Cambridge and he wrote with ease out of the fulness of his knowledge. 'I wrote it for my own amusement.' But there was nothing superficial about it. In the judgement of A. L. Rowse, 'no historian has had such a subtle understanding of her personality as Creighton: something in the sceptical nature of the prelate responded to the nature of the *politique* in her, a woman who was born, as Napoleon said of himself, *un être politique*'.[15]

His qualities as a historian also stand him in good stead in his treatment of the controversial figure of Archbishop Laud. He appreciates fully Laud's concern for the Church and shows that it was the reverse of ignoble and selfish. Laud did much to fix the character of the Church of England and as such deserved the homage of English churchmen. Equally Creighton was not blind to Laud's obvious faults and failings. Laud's zeal, devotion, and conscientiousness excite Creighton's admiration. But Laud failed in sympathy, and his rigidity destroyed his own achievements. Some of Creighton's most succinct historical judgements are dashed off in the course of a private letter. So it is with his estimate of Laud, whom he describes as 'an interesting character, excellent but narrow, with every private virtue and deep religious feeling, but unsympathetic towards others and believing too much in outward organisation—a sort of ecclesiastical policeman at best. Men differ more in real sympathy for their fellows and so in real insight into what is the right thing to do, than either in goodness or wisdom.'[16]

Lytton Strachey was half right when, in his estimate of Creighton as a historian, he wrote: 'In his work a perfectly grey light prevails everywhere.' But he was half wrong too, and when he went on to say 'there is not a single lapse into psychological profundity'[17] his cleverness ran away with him. Of Creighton as historian it might be said that for all his cleverness he never tries to be clever.

4 · THE CHURCH OF ENGLAND

INCREASINGLY as the years went by Creighton conceived his role to be that of expositor of the distinctive features and character of the Church of England. It was not a self-appointed task. In some ways it was thrust upon him by the necessity of having to rule in his diocese and to provide himself, and those over whom he ruled, with clear principles as a basis for his decisions and opinions. But it was also in many ways a congenial task because it made him an apologist for the institution which, above all others, he revered. It was also a role for which he was singularly well fitted by his great historical knowledge, for however much we may rejoice in the continuity of the *Ecclesia Anglicana* and see its beginning in the early centuries of the Christian era, it can only be understood and interpreted in the light of the sixteenth-century Reformation. In this field Creighton's knowledge exceeded that possessed by any other bishop of his time. Forceful, vigorous, and positive though he was in his presentation of the Anglican case, there was no trace of superiority or suggestion that he was laying down the law. But, in speeches and charges, sermons and lectures, he returned over and over again to this theme. He was an advocate who had mastered his brief and a crusader who believed in his cause. At times his advocacy might suggest that he was blind to any other view and his crusading zeal prompted him to an ardour and a hope for the influence of the Church of England on the life of the nation that 'true history' scarcely justified. Though he never removed his glasses except in bed, there was somehow a rosier tint in the lenses when Creighton the bishop spoke about the Church of England than when Creighton the historian wrote about the Papacy. Nevertheless, he remains the truest expositor since Hooker of the character and purpose of the Church of England.

There had been a considerable bias in much historical writing

about the medieval English Church. Creighton recognized this
and criticized those who tried to minimize the dependence of
the English Church on Rome in the Middle Ages. 'The English
Church had good reason for its connexion with Rome, and had
good reason for breaking that connexion, but we gain nothing
by trying to prove either that the connexion never existed, or
was slight, or was foolishly established.'[1] The papal system
owed its existence to the people's will. Public opinion had
welcomed the papal authority. 'People sometimes waste a
great deal of time and pains in explaining away the Papal
power as being the result of all kinds of sacerdotal intrigues and
corruptions, when, as a matter of fact, the Papacy came into
existence and was generally accepted because it represented
what people wanted. . . . This theory of a great spiritual power
guarding over truth and righteousness in every part of Christendom was a splendid idea; only the pity of it was it was so rapidly
lost sight of.'[2] The break with Rome was inevitable and
necessary, but it was made so by the Papacy. 'My arraignment
against the Papacy is that it rendered a violent reformation
necessary because it refused to make a mild and wise one.'

Creighton did not believe in the explosive power of an idea
but in the explosive power of sixpence. Men are moved not by
the ideas in their heads but by the hole in their pockets.

If the Pope would have left off pillaging Germany, I believe
that 'Justification by faith only' would have created only a
languid interest. This is a very low view. I know that we
ought to believe that mighty movements always swayed the
hearts of men. So they have when they made for their
pecuniary interest. But I believe that ideas were always
second thoughts in politics—they were the garb with which
men covered the nudity of their practical desires. I mean that
I can never ask myself first: 'What mighty ideas swelled in
the hearts of men?' but: 'What made men see a chance of
saving sixpence, of gaining sixpence, or escaping from being
robbed of sixpence?' What man was clever enough to devise
a formula round which men could rally for this purpose?[3]

Creighton was always candid. In this passage his candour is heightened by the fact that it is written in the intimacy of a private letter. It helps to explain why he failed to make Luther intelligible. Perhaps it is only another way of saying that the reformation would have been different if it started from a different set of circumstances. He puts the same point in another letter: 'If the Papacy could have put its administration into better order there could have been no reformation, but the new learning would have modified men's attitude towards dogma without causing a breach of the unity of the Church.'[4] Perhaps, too, that is only another way of saying that there would have been no Reformation if there had been a reformation.

In his interpretation of the English Reformation Creighton constantly affirms that the Church of England rests on an appeal to sound learning. An ordination candidate once spoke to Creighton about a dilemma in which he found himself. 'I wish I had a clear answer to the question, "What is the position of the Church of England in Christendom?" I know the claim of the Church of Rome that it is a universal and divinely appointed institution, to which all men must belong. I know the claim of the Greek Church that it preserves the Catholic Faith and sets it forth in ancient form, intelligible to simple people. I do not know any corresponding formula to describe the position of the Church of England.'[5] It was in answer to that dilemma that Creighton affirmed: 'The formula which most explains the position of the Church of England is that it rests on an appeal to sound learning.'[6] In a number of different charges and lectures Creighton reiterated this formula. It became one of his most characteristic affirmations. This was the key to the understanding of the English aspect of the Reformation: 'The great intellectual movement which was sweeping over Europe went on its own lines; it was only accentuated in England by being more frankly accepted there than elsewhere, and probably we should best explain the position of the Church of England if we were to call it "the Church of the New Learning".'[7]

Before the storm of the sixteenth century burst England was already the congenial home of the New Learning. Erasmus described it as 'the abode and stronghold of both virtue and knowledge'. It is this aspect of the English Reformation that appeals so strongly to Creighton. In one of his lectures he contrasts the Church of England with Rome and Geneva:

> Yet where in either of them was there place for the aspirations of the devout scholar, of the man who reverenced liberty, who believed in progressive enlightenment, who longed for an intelligent order of things in which the Christian consciousness should seek for spiritual truth? It was not merely by accident that the great scholar Isaac Casaubon ended his days in England, made happy by the society of Andrewes. It is significant of the temper of the times that the Puritans pelted him with stones in the street when they found he was not a partisan on their side. Still, despite this, Casaubon, with his vast learning and his wide experience of the continent, found peace for his soul in England, which he called 'the isle of the blessed'. In it, despite all drawbacks, still lingered a reverence for knowledge, a love of truth, and a sense of the problems of the future.[8]

The acceptance of Holy Scripture as the sole basis of doctrine did not bind the Anglican Church to any obscurantist position. In Creighton's judgement it promoted historical and scientific inquiry and the acceptance of these methods in the search for truth. The Roman Church, with its greater pretensions, was less effective as a barrier to unbelief in face of the march of Biblical and theological inquiry.

> Intellectually, I see no losses to be set against the gain of a frank acceptance of Holy Scripture as the sole basis of doctrine and Church government, and a recognition that the sense of the gospel has to be determined by strict adherence to logic, grammar and natural science. The modest claim of the Anglican Church to be a witness and keeper of Holy Writ has been fully maintained. The greater pretension of the Roman Church to inherent powers of authoritative interpretation, has not proved so effective a barrier against unbelief. An extensive frontier affords weak places for attack.

The process of slow retreat from untenable positions is hard to accomplish. The imposing appearance of strength vanishes on closer inspection. English theology has shewn a capacity for facing the actual questions which perplex men's minds. It has been strong in its readiness to accept the historic method, and in its desire to obtain scientific results; it has done this in a careful and sober spirit which has made it powerful to mediate between conflicting opinions. The English Church has been especially successful in retaining the allegiance and directing the thought of vigorous minds.[9]

Creighton's understanding of the unique position of the Church of England may be illustrated by the following citation from his Primary Charge in the Diocese of Peterborough, 1894:

Now the Church of England stands in a unique position as regards the whole of this phase of religious development. It did not, like other bodies, cast aside the ancient system of the Church. It was not tempted into the paths of revolution, but followed the safer course of reformation. It did not break the continuity of the historic Church, but with sound learning and spiritual insight proceeded gradually to disentangle what was primitive and Catholic from later accretions, which might be useful or otherwise in themselves, but were to be judged in the first instance with reference, not to their temporary usefulness, but to the standard of Scripture as interpreted by primitive practice. The Church of England, in fact, strove to distinguish between the authority which God for His purpose had conferred on His Church, and that authority which man for his purpose had claimed in God's name. This process was the result of criticism, of careful investigation, accurate inquiry, and impartial weighing of evidence. It did not please enthusiasts on either side; but it was a humble and sincere attempt to learn the lesson which God had taught His Church, and to submit human inventions, however venerable, to the test which God prescribed.

Hence it is that the Church of England stands in a remarkably free attitude towards the progress of human learning. It

D

has nothing to conceal, and shrinks from no inquiry. No religious organisation attaches a higher importance to Holy Scripture, or venerates more highly its authority; but it has never committed itself to any theory concerning the mode in which Scripture was written, or the weight to be attached to it for any other purpose than that of ascertaining all that is necessary to salvation.[10]

In a lecture on 'Biblical Criticism and Anglican Theology' he returns again to a congenial theme.

It has no utterances to explain away, no positions which it is bound to maintain at all hazards. Its great process of reformation was carried out by the recognition of a growth of knowledge. It did not commit the fatal error of erecting a system, strong in an appearance of unchangeable organisation, possessed with an answer to every question, and claiming infallible authority. It laid down decidedly enough the truths of the Catholic faith, it retained every vestige of primitive practice and of primitive organisation; but it left ample room for liberty, and did not pretend to remove from the individual his due share of responsibility. The wisdom of that decision has been abundantly proved by its results. Anglican theology has been distinguished by its sound learning and its penetrating insight. No branch of the Church has made such weighty contributions to theological knowledge since the sixteenth century as has the Church of England. The temper of that Church is admirably adapted to foster theological development on sound lines. I think that Biblical criticism in England is being conducted in a reverential spirit; and though a certain amount of speculation must necessarily be rash, I think that the sense of responsibility is on the whole maintained.[11]

Sound learning demands liberty and an openness of mind; it cannot flourish in any other soil. A wide measure of toleration is a necessary concomitant. There was little toleration anywhere in the sixteenth century but the Anglican settlement was on a broader basis than any other. If the Puritans had had their way the Church settlement would have been on a narrower basis. Creighton appreciates their qualities and the valuable contribution they made to the life of the nation, but the Church of England was fortunate in not being captured by their largely antagonistic zeal.

First of all, the Puritan party were not struggling for toleration, but for mastery. They did not ask for wider option within the system of the Church, but they wished to substitute another system for it. . . .

Taking the largest historical view, I think it must be admitted that England owes a debt of gratitude to those who upheld its struggling Church. We may admire the zeal and the conscientiousness of the Puritans; we may own that they contributed valuable elements to the national character, and largely influenced for good England's subsequent development. But we may say in all fairness that they were not patriotic in their early days, and that their endeavours to make England Calvinistic did not correspond to the best interests of the nation. We may regret that their excellent qualities were deprived of their full influence because they were expressed mainly in resolute antagonism.[12]

The weakness of the Anglican settlement was that in relinquishing the Papal supremacy and rule the Church as a spiritual community gained no greater liberty of action. But in the vexed question of the relations of Church and State that has bedevilled Anglican post-reformation history there is little reason to envy the Roman system.

The Papal headship was abolished and the temporal privileges of that headship transferred to the Crown. Nothing was done to re-establish the organisation of the Church as a self-governing community in spiritual matters. . . . The Church as a spiritual community gained no greater liberty of action. As a consequence, the English Church has shown too great a tendency to Erastianism. Its discipline is defective; it lacks a logical or settled system of jurisdiction. The English Church has been in close relation with the national life. Its demands may not have been so precise as those of the Roman Church, but its pervading influence has been greater. It has had no exact theory of the relations between Church and State; but the exact theory of Rome has never been successful in practice. The English Church may still repair its system in the future; but I doubt whether it has much to learn from the success of the system of the Church of Rome.[13]

It was no good looking in a Rome-ward direction for a solution of the question. 'The Church of Rome is the most complete expression of Erastianism, for it is not a Church at all, but a State in its organisation, and the worst form of state—an autocracy.'[14]

Creighton's passion for liberty and his strong belief that the Church of England was the Church for free men and had a mission both to the nation and to the world made him unsympathetic to the Roman system. 'Romanism still seems something foreign and exotic on English soil, and is alien from the aims and modes of thought of the average Englishman.'[15] The two systems, he believed, produced different characters, as is clear from his comment when he read the life of Cardinal Manning. 'I do not like his character; he was a cold, ambitious man at all times. But the Anglican Church kept his bad qualities down: the Roman Church developed them.'[16]

Creighton frequently compares the two systems at different points. In reply to a correspondent who had complained about the lack of education and training of the English clergy in comparison with the clergy of the Greek and Roman Churches, he comes down heavily on the Anglican side. Imperfect as it is, the situation in the other Churches is infinitely more shocking.

In the Greek Church the majority of the priests are quite ignorant of theology. In the Roman Church the results of the seminary system are that a large proportion are really agnostic or unbelievers, but cannot practically escape as they have been paid for, and have no other opening in life, and dare not go home to poor parents. No system can be perfect; but ours is at least as good as any other: better in that it throws all the responsibility on the individual. Can we do more? People make an ideal of the Roman system. I wish they knew its real working.[17]

His confidence in the Church of England, if it was true to itself, knew no bounds. It was the Church of the future as Rome was the Church of the past.

The function of the Church of England is to be the Church of free men. Its misfortune is that it does not succeed in rising above historical accidents, so as to realise its own great heritage. Its enemy is the Church of Rome; but it ought not to treat its foe with fear, but with kindly regard. The Church of Rome is the Church of decadent peoples: it lives only on its past, and has no future. Borrowing from it may be silly, but it is not dangerous and will pass. The Church of England has before it the conquest of the world. We can only succeed if we gird up our loins with the assurance that the future is ours.[18]

When allowance is made for the rhetorical character of this statement one may still wonder whether the judgement and the prophecy are sound. In the sixty years since his death the Church of England has not grown stronger, though its position in the ecumenical movement may yet be such as to endorse Creighton's prognostications. Creighton also seems to have underestimated the Roman Church's power of adaptation and change.

The Anglican Church has preserved much of the Catholic heritage and not least in its ideals of worship.

The ideal of Anglican worship—Catholic, dignified, simple, free from sensuous excitement, appealing to the whole man, to the head as well as to the heart. Quietly stimulating, invigorating, without calling for undue effort, fostering recollection and gradually heightening the spiritual consciousness. This is expressed and cherished in the historic services of the Cathedral. They set forth in artistic form the ideal of the English Church—the noblest because the most just, the simplest, the most refined and the most spiritual ideal of worship that has been systematised by any branch of the Catholic Church.[19]

Creighton played a prominent part in the controversy about Anglican Orders which culminated in the Bull of Pope Leo XIII (*Apostolicae Curae*, 13 September 1896) in which Anglican Ordinations were pronounced 'absolutely null and utterly void'. It was Creighton who took the initiative in proposing to Archbishop Benson that a reply should be sent. Bishop Wordsworth of Salisbury, Stubbs of Oxford, and Creighton were appointed by the Archbishop to draft the reply. Wordsworth was responsible for the draft but discussed it in detail with Creighton.

The controversy arose out of the well-intentioned efforts of Lord Halifax and others during the years 1894–6 to bring about a better understanding between the Church of England and the Roman Catholic Church. There was a small group of Roman theologians, especially in France, who were anxious to promote closer relations and who thought it might be possible to persuade the Pope to recognize the 'validity' of Anglican Orders. One of them, the Abbé Portal, editor of a French theological review, wrote in eirenic vein under the pen-name P. Dalbus on the subject of Anglican Orders. Lord Halifax appealed to Creighton as well as to the Archbishop of Canterbury for someone to give a sympathetic lead on the Anglican side to Portal's desire for unity. Creighton replied to Lord Halifax appreciating the fairness of Portal 'in outlying points' but clearly recognizing the insuperable obstacle at the heart of the Anglo-Roman controversy.

Any Roman controversy always comes back to the same point: but since the development of Neo-Ultramontanism, controversialists have seemed fairer and more sympathetic, because they could give up the old stories and be fairminded with safety. They had an arm in reserve. When pressed they could always say: 'You are probably quite right: but you acted without the consent of a General Council: therefore your action can never be right.' Now a General Council means to them, a Council summoned by the Pope, and passing decrees which the Pope sanctioned. As the Church of England owed its rise to the necessity for abolishing the papal jurisdiction, it manifestly could not claim the papal consent to that step. Therefore all its proceedings have been invalid. Moreover, they cannot be made valid without the Pope's sanction; and the Pope cannot give that sanction without destroying his own historical claims. It is for this reason that I think the Roman controversy is really barren so far as the Romans are concerned. You may go on well enough for a distance and then comes the blank wall of the papal monarchy. What Episcopacy is to us as regards Nonconformists the Papacy is to the Romans as against us.[20]

It is clear that Creighton was by no means sanguine about the outcome of the private discussions that were proceeding. But Lord Halifax on the Anglo-Catholic side had the idealist's disregard for realities and in the spring of 1895 was engaged in discussions with leading ecclesiastics in Rome, and again appealed by letter to Creighton for a constructive lead from the Anglican side. Creighton's own conception of church unity was federal rather than monarchical. He saw, too, with his practical common sense, the difficulty of arranging for the first step:

Now on the immediate question, the validity of Anglican Orders, I can see the Archbishop's reasons for hesitating. The attitude of Cardinal Vaughan has been very aggressive and exasperating. It is impossible to admit that the Church of England is on trial, or asks for any recognition. There is no doubt amongst us of the validity of our Orders; we are quite satisfied. Roman theologians have denied it and have thereby made the breach. If they thought fit to take any steps to heal it, the effect would doubtless be great. The restoration of the unity of Christendom will be—not by affirming any one of the existing systems as universal, but by a federation.[21]

The Church of England could certainly not go cap-in-hand to the Pope. Creighton sums up his letter to Lord Halifax by saying: 'If any recognition of our position were given by the Pope, it would be of enormous use: but we cannot ask for it without putting ourselves in the wrong. We have done nothing to invalidate our Orders: Rome has wantonly denied them in the past. We at our worst have never unchurched Rome: latterly we have almost been too kind to her.'[22]

On 22 April 1895, Pope Leo XIII issued an encyclical letter, *Ad Anglos* (To the English). It was offensive to many people for what was thought to be its patronizing tone and was dismissed by some as insolent in its failure to recognize the existence of the Church of England. Creighton, on the other hand, received it in a friendly and sympathetic spirit. He spoke of it at his Diocesan Conference: 'The fact that Leo XIII should have issued a letter to the English people is at least a manifestation of goodwill. I do not like to criticise that letter in detail. It was addressed to the English people, probably as an indication that no answer was expected. From one at least it shall receive none. I think we may accept a token of friendliness and of Christian sympathy in the spirit which it expresses.'[23]

In Creighton's judgement it was premature to discuss methods of reunion. There was a lot of weeding in the garden to be done first.

> The first step must necessarily be to make us all more deeply conscious of the intellectual, the historical, and the sentimental differences which keep us asunder. But intercourse, friendly feeling, and reflection will enable us or our children to remove misunderstanding, to dissolve the veil of sentiment, to go behind the prejudices created by mistakes and misdoings of the past, to separate what is accidental and temporary from what is essential, to discover the real importance of the points which keep us asunder, to raise controversy above passion, to discuss principles without being troubled by the thoughts of temporary loss or gain.[24]

Against this background of events and Creighton's own pacific, if realistic, approach to them the gratuitous publication of the Papal Bull condemning Anglican Orders as 'absolutely null and utterly void' could only seem to Creighton a slap in the face. His immediate reaction is expressed in a letter he wrote the day following the publication of the Bull. 'The Pope of

Rome has been at his old games; and doubtless Vaughan and Co. are chuckling. I think their victory will not profit them even in this world. It will entail on them a very long purgatory in the next. I wonder if they have provided themselves adequately with Indulgences. But for the present and for the long future this will end the leanings of the foolish towards the Western Church and will bring the Eastern Church into greater prominence.'[25]

Though he was disappointed and regretted deeply the publication of the Bull, Creighton could not have been altogether surprised at the turn of events. He had consistently asserted that the crux of the problem of the relation of the English Church with the Roman Church was the necessity of submission to papal jurisdiction. All the Roman arguments resolved themselves into this. It was not primacy or recognition but absolute submission to papal jurisdiction which was the one necessity for Catholicity according to the modern Roman view. Creighton did not believe that Leo XIII held this view, but that he was a prisoner of his own system. 'An institution grasps at power, because so many officials depend on its existence. This was the *fons et origo mali* in the sixteenth century. The revolt was against an extortionate Curia, and the Pope upheld it because he could not escape. This is the real hindrance still.'[26]

Some might argue that the Roman claims were not so rigid and unchangeable as is often supposed. Creighton knew this only too well but it strengthened rather than weakened his opposition to the Roman system.

Englishmen will not be moved by the argument that Roman formulae were capable of being explained away. Of course we know that Rome's method has been one of accommodation and that the practices vary immensely, and that her formulae are held in various senses. In fact, Rome has always followed, and has not directed popular religious opinion. This is just where the average Englishman takes alarm. He believes in truth: he wants not the widest but the truest statement:

he believes in raising and educating the people, not in finding room for their fancies and sentiments. There is somewhere the essential difference between the Latin and Teutonic mind to be got over. It was this which asserted itself in the sixteenth century. The Reformation was the effect not the cause of a breach which had slowly grown: and the Teuton has been justified by its results.[27]

The impossibility of any co-operation with the Roman Catholic Church has always tended to create antagonistic feelings in the minds of Anglicans. Creighton was clearly no exception. 'Scratch an Englishman and find a Protestant' was true in his case. The whole Roman system, its mind and temper, was anathema to him. His relations with other dissenters were quite different. As Vicar of Embleton he gave offence to some of the neighbouring clergy by being present at the induction service of the local Presbyterian minister. As Bishop of Peterborough he expressed gratified surprise that none of his clergy nor the church papers wrote remonstrating with him when he sent a message of goodwill and greetings to the President of the Congregational Union meeting at Leicester. His relations with nonconformists were at all times courteous. But he had no time for undenominationalism. 'It leads to the destruction of Christianity as a religion and converts it into a sort of moral philosophy, which rests upon the notion that the "spiritual" man is merely the "natural" man at his best, and does not realise that the "spiritual" man is a "new creature".' He was quick to appreciate the work of the nonconformist churches and to value the contribution they had made to English life and character. Let all work together when they could. 'I should say that we can join all men in work which is *hortative* or *preventive*; when the subject is edifying we must do it on our own lines.'[28] But undenominationalism was simply 'as much fruit and as little root as possible'.[29]

Creighton lectured on the 'Protestant Sects' at Cambridge and drew out the particular contribution which each of the main nonconformist churches had made to English Christianity.

'English nonconformity has great memories. All its various forms correspond to some genuine need of the time in which it arose. Each embodies some great truth which was once overlooked or neglected.'[30]

When he lectured on the Congregationalists he spoke with sympathetic understanding and charity though, in his judgement, the Congregationalists had sacrificed the historic Church which the Anglican Reformers were at pains to preserve. The great virtues of the Congregationalists were their regard for individual responsibility and the integrity of conscience, but at the end of the lecture the Anglican apologist in him, which was always rising to the surface, took over.

We of the Church of England have increasing reason to rejoice that our country, in its time of trial, preserved the immemorial heritage of the Catholic Church. The days are past when it can be regarded as a matter of policy or convenient arrangement. It has become the object of our deepest reverence, of our most passionate regard. We can point, as to the witness of God's presence, to the marvellous recuperative power which it has shown and is showing; to its capacity to adapt itself to altered circumstances and conditions of life and thought; to its willingness to learn truths which it has mistakenly overlooked; to learn from Congregationalists that regard for individual responsibility, that sense of the integrity of conscience to maintain which their forefathers suffered and died. In spite of all its faults the Church of England is the historic Church which has influenced and is influencing the world by its testimony to the abiding presence of the Lord, not in the heart of one and another who here and there in scattered congregations assemble in His name, but in the vast body of Christian men dispersed throughout the world, who are what they are through union with Him in His visible Church, the true fostering mother of us all.[31]

Reunion with the nonconformist churches was not a practical issue in Creighton's day. He was never concerned with any question of reunion, and there is little on the subject in his

writings. But he saw the possibility of a Commonwealth of
Churches in which differences remained but were superseded
by a common purpose. 'I can conceive of a Christian Commonwealth, consisting of bodies of believers each with opinions of
their own about matters of organisation, understanding one
another and respecting one another, yet conscious of a common
purpose which transcends all human methods.'[32]

The *via media* of the Church of England was for Creighton
the ideal, and *via media* was to be understood in the sense in
which Aristotle defined virtue as being a mean state between
excess and defect. But the most characteristic feature of the
English Church and that which distinguished it among the
churches of Christendom was the balance it achieved between
law and liberty. Creighton once scribbled in pencil on the back
of an envelope a few sentences which aptly summarize the
position as he saw it.

'The work of the Church of England is to maintain truth
held according to liberty yet with order.'

'The Church of Rome cares for truth and order but subordin-
ates truth.'

'The nonconformists care for truth and liberty but truth is
dissolved into opinion.'

'It is hard to maintain the three together, but this constitutes
England's work.'[33]

Freedom and order must be somehow combined. Toleration
was an important principle, but there must be limits to its
application. 'Tolerance is not only a moral virtue, it must have
an intellectual basis. The question is: How much can be
comprehended in the Church of England? I remember a
remark of a Frenchman, talking about modern liberalism.
*"Ils confondent le droit de l'individu d'être libre avec la nécessité de
l'institution d'être quelque chose."* The Church of England may be
tolerant, but it must be something.'[34]

Creighton returns to his favourite theme—the principles of
freedom and order—and to his hopes and ideals for the Church
of England in an address at Sion College in the last year of
his life.

I am not ashamed to call myself an enthusiastic and fanatical Anglican. It is as an ecclesiastical system that I value the Church of England. Its system seems to me infinitely higher than any other, and it is for that very reason that it appears so defective, because the higher its aims the larger are the demands it makes upon its members, and consequently its ideal can seldom or never be realised. This is the very defect of Christianity itself, which always stands at a disadvantage, so far as the consistency of the lives of its adherents is concerned, when compared with other religions, because of the almost intolerable burden of responsibility which it throws upon the shoulders of those who profess it. . . . There are two principles of the highest possible order which are always at war with one another, the principle of freedom, which is necessary to the individual, and the principle of order, which is necessary to the society of which the individual is a member; there is always a struggle between the sense of freedom and the sense of discipline; to construct a system which represents the rightful claims both of freedom and order is extremely difficult. It is easy to construct a system in which either prevails. In the Church of England we have a system which equally respects the claims of order and the claims of liberty; this demands some intellectual knowledge as well as moral training and discipline. . . . Here is the great opportunity of the Church of England fully to realise its position, and for its members to act up to their obligations . . . it offers infinitely the greatest possibilities for the growth of human intelligence, of the moral sense of men, of individual freedom within the order of a divinely constituted society. . . . As a missionary agency it has unique and unparalleled opportunities.[35]

Creighton had no doubt about the Catholicity of the Church of England and its retention of essential Catholic order and doctrine. Nor was this simply an accident of history occasioned by the demands of political convenience. It represented the deliberate convictions and intentions of the Anglican reformers. But, while stressing the Catholicity of the Anglican Church, he believed that the 'continuity' argument had been overdone, and that the essence of Anglicanism was to be found not so much in its continuity with the past as in the character of the changes made at the Reformation. It was the difference from the past rather than the likenesses that needed stressing. 'The "continuity" theory has been overdone. In the sense of continuity of organisation it is true; but this has been made to carry a vast amount, which must be disentangled. The changes made in England were changes in spirit, temper, appeal to learning, and assertion of liberty. This must be more adequately recognised.'[36]

Creighton was too much of a realist to be unaware of the perils inherent in all powerful institutions and not least in the Church. The warnings of history were always in his mind.

The danger to which all institutions are exposed is that they are founded for the good of men, but as they become powerful they tend to exist primarily for their own good. Ease of organisation, order and regularity are what every institution inevitably aims at. It insensibly demands that men should take the form in which they can most easily be organised and dealt with. This is the danger which has always beset the Western Church. It is hardly an exaggeration to say that the history of that Church is of a series of struggles to keep it a humane institution. The central mechanism of the Church always tended to become abstract, to grow out of genuine contact with life. Great movements towards monasticism, and still more the simple methods of the Friars, brought it back again from time to time. But gradually the central mechanism laid its benumbing hand upon these reforming movements, and checked their vitality. As the fabric became more stately, it lost in effective power. When its organisation had been forged into apparently irrefragable strength, it was found to be intolerable.

This is a warning never to be forgotten. The medieval Church fell, because it had ceased to influence human life through its excessive endeavours to accommodate itself to its needs; because it expanded its system to meet the requirements of feeble consciences, which grew feebler the more they were tended; because it undertook to do so much for men's souls, that men felt they were losing all consciousness that their souls were after all their own.[37]

The history of the Western Church was also a warning to the Church of England. It, too, had to struggle to remain a humane institution. If the sacerdotalists had their way men might begin to wonder again if their souls were really their own. Creighton was alive to this point. 'I deplore all demonstrations of clerical arrogance as being the temptations to which undisciplined zeal is exposed, and which constitute a real danger.' But so far as the Church of England was concerned Creighton was both a realist and an optimist. His realism sprang from his good sense and his wide historical knowledge; his optimism sprang from his understanding of the basis of the English Church and his passionate belief in the English character. The sacerdotalists might threaten the Church but he had no fear of any permanent harm from eccentric restlessness because the English conception of liberty was too strong to be set aside. The village Hampdens would see us through. If only men would take the trouble to understand the character of the English Church then it would be seen for what he believed it to be, the best form of Church that man had ever devised, the most consonant with the divine intention, and as such the Church of the future. No English ecclesiastic would have been more ready than Creighton to echo George Herbert's sentiment in his poem, *The British Church*:

> But dearest Mother, (what those miss),
> The mean, thy praise and glory is,
>   And long may be.
>
> Blessed be God, whose love it was
> To double-moat thee with His grace,
>   And none but thee.

It was the one subject which moved Creighton to a rhetorical flourish.

> We tend, I think, to make too many apologies for the supposed defects of the Church of England; its want of discipline; its absence of positive definition on many points; its large latitude of opinion. To me it seems that the Church of England is the only religious organisation which faces the world as it is, which recognises the actual facts, and works for God, in God's own way. ... The Church of England is rigid in maintaining necessary truth, and is careful to draw the line between what is necessary and what is matter for expediency. ... I trust that the time is past when anyone wishes, for uniformity's sake, to narrow the limits of the English Church. ... Its proudest boast is that it faces the world as it is, and faces it simply and straightforwardly. It has no reservations, nothing which it need explain away. The treasures of the past history of the Church are open to its children, and they are free to adapt them to the needs of their souls, provided they do not force as obligatory what has been deliberately left to the responsibility of the individual. The aspirations and ideas of the present, in politics, in science, in thought, have no terrors for the Church of England, for its hold of vital truth has never been encumbered by the rubbish of falling scaffoldings and tottering buttresses, which threaten to drag the main building into ruin. The Church of England faces the world as it is, knowing that the world-spirit is strong and operative in many forms, resolute in maintaining God's truth. But it draws a clear line between God's truth and man's means of expressing it, however noble and beautiful they may be. God's truth set forth in accordance with primitive practice, that is the position of the English Church.[38]

Creighton's intense veneration for the system of the English Church stemmed partly from the fact that the system was based firmly on broad principles and was not tied to a meticulous and intricate Code of Canon Law. It was not a 'Canonist' version of Christianity. This, he believed, suited the English temperament, especially in modern times. Here was a further point of contrast between the English and Roman system. An all-embracing Code of Canon Law can only be tolerable and workable when there are large powers of dispensation. This has been the practice of the Roman Church. As a result of this flexible system of dispensation legislation was not hampered by any fear that enactments would have to be carried out. Law had less and less relation to life. Creighton enlarged on this theme in a paper read to the Church Historical Society in 1895:

> The ingenuity of Canonists was unfettered by any thought of the consequences of their conclusions, as it was comparatively easy to escape those consequences if desirable. It is of little practical purpose to study the Canon Law and point to its precepts as the law of the Church, binding for all times, if not revoked. As practically applied, it was an ideal system, with little relation to life. It was a triumph of logical ingenuity which everyone regarded as admirable. Men in the Middle Ages loved law, and could not have too much of it—on paper. Our ideas have changed in modern times and we dislike to live under regulations which are not observed by the community.[39]

There seemed to be no limit to the persistent extension of this system of accommodation, and herein, Creighton believed, lay the explanation of the moral force behind the protests of the sixteenth century. A system of dispensations is repugnant to the Church of England. But there is no practical alternative if a tight and comprehensive system of Canon Law is imposed and legalized. A Code of Canons is best thought of as a storehouse of good advice. Creighton asserts that the most important fact in the history of the medieval Church is that the 'accumulation of good advice was ingeniously constructed into a legal system and administered as such'.[40] In freeing itself from this 'Canonist' version of Christianity the Church of England achieved a new spirit and temper. It was his appreciation of this emancipation that made Creighton a devoted and fanatical Anglican.

E

5 · THE CHURCH AND THE NATION

'I AM not ashamed to own that I am an Englishman first and a Churchman afterwards.'[1] Creighton received a post-humous rap over the knuckles from Hensley Henson for this remark. Certainly it was a reckless utterance which Creighton found it hard to explain away. Henson said it was 'either a mere platitude, for every man must be born before he can be baptized, or the very essence of spiritual treason'.[2] But Creighton was an Englishman first because being an Englishman was for him a religion, and, as he understood it, a very good religion.

Most of Creighton's epigrammatic and explosive statements, such as 'The Catholic Church must go into the waste-paper-basket', were made in private conversation or in intimate personal letters. His remark about being an Englishman first and a churchman afterwards could claim no such privilege. It was made openly in the course of a speech at a public meeting. Not surprisingly, it gave some offence at the time, but, rightly construed, it is the key to the understanding of his conception of a national Church. No doubt he overstressed the appeal to the great English tradition, but the offensive epigram must be seen in its context. 'But to my mind', he went on to say, 'Church and State are not contradictory things. Church and State are the nation looked at from different points of view. The nation looked at from the secular side is the State, looked at from the religious side it is the Church, and separation between the two is impossible.'

This identity of the English Church with the English nation imbued his whole being. The Church of England was the State on its Godward side. He could not conceive of it as a sect or remnant type of church, or as an institution set against the State, nor could he have been interested in such a church. He exploded with his offensive epigram to oppose a narrow and sectarian view of the Christian religion. He was no ecclesiastic in the narrow sense, and the Church of England meant more to him because it was national rather than because it was part of a universal Catholic Church. But there was no necessary contradiction between a national Church, as Creighton conceived it, and the One Holy Catholic and Apostolic Church. Its local name signified that it consisted of the members of that Church living in a particular country. The national Church had no power to change the creeds or the early organization of the Universal Church. But it had the right, and indeed the duty, to determine how the Christian faith could be best set forth and, for that purpose, it could regulate rites, ceremonies, usages, and discipline according to its own wisdom and its experience of the needs of the people. The Church in England was always understood to serve the people in England. It was for this end that the Church *in* England became the Church *of* England. Creighton always emphasized the necessity of the Church representing the national life. The Church must be the guardian, the educator, and the exponent of the national conscience. 'The Church sets forth the fundamental truths on which man's life is based; the State attempts to organize the life of the community in the most satisfactory way. There must frequently be differences about embodying principles in practice. The Church must frequently criticize proposals of the State. Church and State alike work for the good of the community, but they begin at different ends. The State is willing to redress particular grievances, the Church is upholding general principles.'[3]

This theme finds a place in many of Creighton's public addresses and charges. At the Exeter Church Congress in 1894 he defined the State as 'the community which is concerned with the arrangements of the common life' and the Church as 'the community concerned with setting forth the principles on which all life rests'. After these definitions he proceeds: 'Why should not Church and State exist side by side? For a long time they did and nobody thought about doubting the necessity of the arrangement, but then something was discovered that is called liberty. A good many people nowadays regard liberty as

a kind of fad. I for my part think that liberty is the most
valuable principle that has ever been discovered.'[4] He went
on to show that the Church and the State had to apply the
principle of liberty in different ways. The State allowed the
game of politics to be played like a game of cricket. The two
sides bat in turn. Religious liberty had to be promoted in a
different way. The solution found to the problem of religious
liberty was to have a National Church and, by the side of it,
voluntary religious societies. He proceeded to consider the
objections to an established Church. It would not do to point
to the example of America and the colonies. 'We must stand
by what we have inherited, and it would be the greatest blow
to civilisation not only in England, but in Europe generally, if
the ancient historic land of England abandoned its connexion
with religion.'[5]

For Creighton, English churchmanship was a form of
national service. His anti-Roman bias comes out again in his
treatment of this aspect of the theme. To join the Roman
Church was to stand aside from the main stream of the religious
life of the country; it was almost a form of disloyalty:

> The English people are committed to the care of the English
> Church. From time to time they express their opinion about
> the mode of teaching which is applied to them. The Church
> of Rome is a small body in England, which stands in no
> relation to the religious life of the nation. It is quite im-
> possible that any considerable number of Englishmen should
> be Roman Catholics. To join yourself to that Church is
> simply to stand on one side and cut yourself off from your
> part in striving to do your duty for the religious future of
> your country. That duty may be at times difficult and un-
> pleasant. Duty generally is so. But we must not shirk it on
> that account, or try to find peace for ourselves by standing on
> one side.[6]

Creighton was an Englishman to the core, but his dedicated
patriotism did not make him blind to the defects of the English
character: 'Englishmen above all men refuse to think things

out'—a thought which he also expresses in other forms. 'Most Englishmen have no mind at all, but only hereditary obstinacy.' And again: 'An Englishman is not only without ideas but he hates an idea when he sees it.'[7] In spite of all this Creighton drew his strength from the sympathy he had with his fellow Englishmen and his respect for the English character and tradition.

Figgis maintained that Creighton's study of the Conciliar Movement had a great bearing on his conception of the Church of England. This period (roughly speaking, 1378–1450) had been little studied by English scholars but was really more rewarding of study than many more picturesque epochs of church history. Creighton became a master in this little-known field. The Conciliar Movement was not important for any practical success. It was, in fact, a failure. But the ideas which animated it were, in a broad sense, the ideas that form the *raison d'être* of the Church of England as against Ultramontanism on the one hand and individualistic Protestant sectarianism on the other.

The claims of Rome that we are but a sect among other sects would be justified if the Conciliar Movement was based on a fundamental falsehood. Roughly speaking the ideals of Gerson and his congeners were those of a reformed Episcopal communion with nationalism recognised in the Church as a real thing, with a constitution limiting the dangers of centralised bureaucracy (the real evil of Rome far more than mere monarchical government)—in a word with federalism in the Church preserving the unity of the whole while securing the independence of the parts. The failure of that scheme is one of the most tragic facts in the history of the world and was as direct a cause of the Reformation as the despotism of Louis XIV was the real origin of the Great Revolution. Now Creighton's task in later years was to apply this truth to modern problems. There arose in the Church a party small, for the most part un-learned, but intensely enthusiastic, whose ideals were purely those of Latin Christianity, and whose conception of the Church was in the last resort ultramontane.

Creighton saw earlier than most people that the real question at issue was not whether the Church of England had done this or that in the past, not even whether it had the right to do this and that, but whether there was a Church of England at all.[8]

Could there be National Churches with a divine mission? There was no doubt in Creighton's mind about this. The Church of England was such a church with its own rights and powers and a life of its own. This was the essence of the Conciliar Movement and Creighton's advocacy of the rights of nationalism within the Church and his repudiation of mere individualism drew strength from his unrivalled knowledge of this half-forgotten period of church history.

Strong though he was in his advocacy of the National Church, and distressed as he was by those who, in his judgement, were undermining its influence in the life of the nation, he knew that the only weapon of defence was patience and the only weapon of attack was persuasion.

Here, however, as elsewhere, his respect for liberty preserved him from mistakes. Convinced of the truth of his main principles, imbued as he was perhaps more strongly than any thinker since Hooker with the genius of the Church of England, despising the frivolity and ignorance with which the Latinisation of the Church was being pushed forward, and deeply opposed to the legalist conception of religion in general, and to Canonist Christianity in particular, Creighton's strong hand alone prevented an outburst of the persecuting spirit which would have left the Church shorn of some of its best elements.[9]

Creighton was an Establishment man to his finger-tips. The constitutional link between Church and State in England was a source of untold blessing to both partners in a common enterprise. Any suggestion of a severance in that partnership filled him with gloom. 'That an ancient nation like England should deliberately repudiate any organic connexion between the basis of its national life and the profession of the Christian faith seems to me to be a calamity which could never be repaired.'[10] So intense were his feelings on the subject of disestablishment that it became the one topic on which he might be said to have forfeited his sovereign impartiality. It was also the one topic that could sometimes give a jingoistic ring to his public utterances. 'It is one of the proud boasts of Englishmen at present that they can say that they are Englishmen first and that nothing stands between them and allegiance to their country. But it will be very different if the Church of England is disestablished; then there will be many who will be constrained to say that they are Churchmen first and only Englishmen afterwards.'[11]

The value of the Establishment was one of the lessons Creighton drew from history. In one of his church history lectures at Worcester, after showing how the Church had come to the aid of the State in its deplorable condition in the reign of Stephen, he asserted that such a contingency might recur. This was one of his strong arguments against disestablishment. 'It would destroy an organisation the importance of which only those could understand who had meditated on the general lines of English history, an organisation identical with the national life, as it is and as it might be, and showing itself at a crisis a very great safeguard. The Church can do work which the State cannot do, and untie knots which the State cannot untie.'[12]

A man of liberal sympathies in politics, Creighton favoured the onward march of democracy and the extension of the franchise. But there was a danger that the appetite for legislation might become a substitute for good administration and statesmanship. 'The fault that I have to find is that everybody is concerned with proposing legislative changes of no importance and no one cares for capable administration and wise statesmanship. These things made England and they are becoming lost arts. If the coming democracy is going to turn Parliament into a large Vestry, if reforms of the House of

Lords and disestablishment of the Church are to be the object of legislative energy, the future can only be disastrous.'[13] In the 1885 election he used his influence to ensure that disestablishment should be removed from the Cambridge candidate's programme as not being a practical question. 'In Cambridge the liberal candidate is a Quaker. I joined in demanding that he should declare that during this Parliament he would vote for no Bill or resolution favouring disestablishment. He agreed as a fair-minded man: then I was full on his side.'[14] But Creighton was no rigid and obstinate supporter of the *status quo*. In the same year he was a moving spirit in a small group of Cambridge dons who prepared a memorial to the Archbishop and Bishops on the subject of church reform. Questions of patronage and church discipline were mentioned, but the pressing need was for changes in the constitution and government of the Church that would admit laymen to a real share in the control of church affairs.

Disestablishment was no cure for the ills of the Church; it was the establishment which held the Church of England together. Two months before he died, when he was making up his mind to veto the proposed prosecution of two incumbents in his diocese, Creighton wrote to Lord Edward Churchill: 'You regard disestablishment as a "remedy for our present troubles". I wish I could share this confidence. Any synodical body would be less liberal than our present system, and the ejection of offenders against rules would be infinitely easier. If we were disestablished at present we could not possibly hold together.'[15]

The nonconformist cry that the State should not interfere in matters of religion seemed to Creighton disingenuous and dangerous. He speaks at some length on this and other aspects of the call for disestablishment in his Primary Charge to the Clergy and Churchwardens of the Diocese of Peterborough in 1894:

There was a time in England when the State decided that national unity was only possible on the basis of religious uniformity. The State failed to secure uniformity, but discovered that outward uniformity was no longer necessary for political security, and consequently withdrew from the attempt to secure it. The nonconformists, finding themselves driven by the State in a direction in which they conscientiously objected to go, raised a cry that the State ought not to meddle with religion. Their contention was absolutely true, so far as is meant that the State ought not to exercise any coercive power over the conscience of its subjects. It is absolutely untrue when it is pressed to the conclusion, that, to secure this result, the State should be stripped of all connection with the religious life of the nation. Yet this is the logical extreme which is being pursued. It is even erected into an axiom.[16]

Creighton's passionate approval of the Church and State connexion was partly due to his conception of the divine vocation of the State. There was nothing unclean about it, as the enthusiasts for disestablishment seemed to suggest:

I can think of nothing so tending to debase the ideal of the State as talk about freeing the Church from the bondage of the State. This representation of the State as something inherently unholy, something stifling to spiritual aspirations, something from which the high-minded man longs to be delivered, is very dangerous teaching, and indeed is not seriously meant. But Disestablishment, or, as I prefer to call it, the repudiation of a Christian basis of the State, would go far to give real vitality to such opinions. Deplorable as this result would be, I do not see on what grounds it could be deprecated by those who rashly raise so large an issue to gain such a trivial advantage.[17]

Creighton would not object to being called an Englishman and a churchman in that order. They were one and the same person. There was nothing of the ecclesiastical temper about him.

It would be a worthy object of our endeavour to change

the sense which attaches in current literature to the phrase 'the ecclesiastical temper'. Surely we know no temper, save the temper of our Lord. It is because I fervently believe that the present position of the Church of England, in its relation to the State and to Society, affords a splendid opportunity for bringing religion to bear upon every relation in life, that I deplore the possibility of any change. The influence of the Church, its responsibility, its sense of a mission, these are inherent in its own nature. Nothing can either add to or take from them. But the sphere and method of its influence must depend upon the nature of its relationship to the community in which it works. My contention is that the relationship, which now exists in England, is practically in accordance with the genius of English institutions, and is fruitful of great promise for the future.[18]

6 · THE OFFICE AND WORK OF A BISHOP

IT has been said that there is only one spiritual disaster for a clergyman greater than that of thinking that he should be made a bishop, and that is that he should have been made a bishop. Creighton was no climbing cleric. Some of his closest friends caused him embarrassment by predicting an episcopal career for him. On one occasion at Worcester, walking by the river and referring to these prognostications, he said to his wife: 'I should like to put a special petition in the Litany that I might be saved from becoming a Bishop, and the worst of it is I believe I should make quite a good Bishop.'[1] There was little doubt that with his combination of learning and other gifts, if the opportunity came his way, he would fill the office with remarkable distinction. But he did not seek it and only a few weeks before his nomination to Peterborough he had written to Figgis: 'I hear that Westcott is quite pleased with episcopal functions, but has not opened a book since he left Cambridge. Such is the pressure of practical life: it is terrible to contemplate such a condition.'[2] It was not long before Creighton was to be in the same plight and to be writing of himself: 'There was a time—strange as it may seem, when I was able to read a book; that has faded into the dim past; but I look back with pleasure and delight upon that time.'[3]

Too much can be made of the loss of opportunity for original scholarship: the loss was more than offset by the gain. He had a larger sphere of influence and he filled the episcopal office as to the manner born. At Peterborough his life was arduous but comparatively untroubled. There were 675 parishes in the diocese, and from the outset he was anxious to go everywhere and see everything for himself. He had a strict rule never to act as patron of a bazaar, but in other things he was ready to put himself out. He was frank and easy in manner and some thought him unguarded in his conversation. At first he surprised and puzzled people simply by being so accessible to everybody, for this was a novelty to them. In his first public speech at Northampton he likened a bishop's life to that of a commercial traveller—always going somewhere with a bag in his hand.

Life was always strict and simple—even severe—in the Creighton household, and when the house became a palace simplicity was still the rule. The Bishop graduated to first class on the railways. More work could be done that way. But his personal life remained simple. It was too arduous to be otherwise. Extravagance requires leisure for its exercise; self-indulgence goes with indolence and Creighton was a stranger to excess. In home life he was not communicative about diocesan affairs and rarely conversed with the family about official business. Mrs. Creighton was an able and formidable person in her own right; but there was no Mrs. Proudie in the Palace at Peterborough or Fulham.

The high quality of Creighton's official correspondence, as also of his private letters, is largely due to the fact that he wrote all letters of importance himself. Dictation is the ruination of the art of letter-writing, and Creighton dealt with a mountain of correspondence with a minimum of secretarial help. He was not a popular man in the sense in which that word is sometimes applied to clerics. No one would have called him the people's bishop as no one would have called him a man's man. He was never concerned to make himself popular. His range of interests and abilities was too wide for him simply to be a popular and lovable figure. He was revered, respected, and sometimes feared. His own comment on what a clergyman should be is an apt summary of what he was. 'The strength of a clergyman's position lies in the fact that he belongs to no class and to no party. It is his duty to consider only the general welfare and seek out the principles on which it rests.'[4] In the university he had been an arresting teacher; in the diocese he saw his mission in a different way. 'I feel my function in life is changed. It is no longer to teach but to edify. I have no longer to startle people out of self-complacency, but to be kindly, sympathetic, humble, and helpful. Yes, *servus servorum Dei*—that much abused title needs to be revived in its deepest sense.'[5]

The clearest insight into Creighton's conception of the office and work of a bishop in the Church of England can be found in his penetrating study of Archbishop Laud. It is one of the best short accounts of Laud's policy and character, revealing both his strength and weakness. 'Two things must be kept distinct, Laud's conception of the Church of England and the means which he took to embody this conception.'[6] The one was noble, the other ignominious. 'It is not hard to have a noble end; the difficulty lies in working it out by worthy means. We can never learn this lesson enough. It is the great moral lesson which history teaches, and only when this lesson is clearly taught does history teach aright.'[7] Laud took the policeman view rather than the pastor view of the episcopal office. This was the essential limitation of Laud's view of episcopacy— it lacked the pastoral element. Creighton recognized this, and the pastoral function took precedence over all others in his own episcopal policy. Not so with Laud:

He completely identified the Church with the State. He knew, to quote his own words, 'that my order as a Bishop, and my power of jurisdiction, is by Divine Apostolical right, and unalterable (for aught I know) in the Church of Christ'; but he took no other view of his right to exercise his office, either of power or jurisdiction, than as derived from the Crown, and exercisable according to law. He does not seem to have thought of the paternal jurisdiction inherent in his office, and independent of anything that the State could confer. The loss of this conception did more to confuse men's minds about the nature of the Church than any of Laud's measures did to make it clear. His action did much to stereotype the view of a bishop's office as an executor of national laws, passed through motives of expediency, and founded on other than theological reasons. This was the view which rendered Episcopacy unpopular, which gave strength to

Nonconformity, and involved the system of the Church in current politics. If Laud had conferred with his clergy and striven to guide and influence them by the authority of his Episcopal office, if he had exhorted his suffragans to do the same, his revival might not have gone so far, but it would assuredly have rested on a firmer basis. It would have been ecclesiastical in a true sense, and would have associated discipline with the system of the Church rather than the laws of State. If the Church of England claimed to refer to primitive antiquity for its belief and practice, surely its episcopal government should be carried on with reference to primitive methods. As it was, Laud's exercise of authority was an anomaly.[8]

An appropriate sub-title for Creighton's analysis of Laud's episcopal policy might well be 'How not to be a Bishop'. Laud chose to work through power rather than through influence, to impose his policy rather than to persuade men that it was right. Creighton also draws another lesson from Laud's disastrous methods. It was the lesson of patience and sympathetic concern in all spiritual work.

When much work has to be done a man is bound to be niggardly of his time; he becomes impatient of details; and he who would work for God must learn never to be in a hurry, must curb his natural impatience, must remember how tenderly God has dealt with him, must regard no time wasted which composes differences or removes scruples, which cheers, consoles, or convinces. . . . It is impossible not to admit that, as years went on, and the burden of work increased, Laud failed in temper and discretion, grew more arbitrary and less hopeful.[9]

These were the lessons that Creighton took to heart. They helped to fashion his own conception of the work and office of a bishop in the Church of England. He spoke of one aspect of it at a Diocesan Conference: 'There is one thing I should like to say as regards my conception of the Episcopal office. It is that all the clergy of this diocese are alike the objects of my personal concern and my personal care, however mistaken I may think them to be in some points, and whether I personally agree with them or not.'[10] On another occasion, when addressing a deputation of the Church Association, he expresses succinctly the function of a bishop. 'In early times great difficulties beset the Church of England because the bishops were regarded as policemen. A bishop has two jurisdictions—the pastoral and the judicial, but his judicial functions are distinctly second to his pastoral.'[11]

A bishop had to preserve unity between congregations. That was the original purpose of the episcopal office. He had to promote the general welfare of the Church, to seek out the principles on which it rested, to serve noble ends by noble means, to be patient, and to rely on influence rather than power. That was the only way to be *servus servorum Dei*. It was the way Creighton followed in all his episcopal administration.

It was no easy task, as Creighton was to find. The divisions of conscientious opinion within the Church of England were such that the solidarity of the Church was continually threatened and the Bishop who strove to bring all together in 'one holy bond of truth and peace, of faith and charity' was overwhelmed by the burden of his office and finally broken by it. He valued the comprehensiveness of the English Church and the differences of belief and practice found within it. He was ready to show sympathy to all on condition that they were loyal to the principles of the Church of England.

This general conception of the solidarity of the Church is one that I have very strongly in my mind; there is nothing that I more earnestly desire than to bring together all members of the Church; I am bound to say that I cannot speak in a melancholy way of what we sometimes call 'our unhappy divisions'. I must tell you frankly that I rejoice in the breadth and width of the Church of England as it is; I recognise the enormous advantages which every different school of thought contributes towards the general spread of those eternal principles of truth in which we are all interested. It is quite clear, in such a country as this in which we live amongst the social, political and intellectual conditions under which our lot is cast—it is quite clear that no one set of opinions, no one form of Divine service, no one particular way of presenting religious ideas, will universally prevail. It is impossible to think that the English people will be dragooned into absolute uniformity about everything; they will have differences of opinion about the forms of their services as about everything else, and I think it my duty, as bishop of this Diocese, to show my sympathy with all forms of service and all forms of religious zeal, which are loyally in accordance with the principles of the Church of England.[12]

This insistence on loyalty to the principles of the Church of England became for Creighton an axiom of his episcopal administration. He was ready to interpret it widely as he was ready to apply it patiently. But he would not abandon it.

Though it could sometimes seem that divisions are deepest over trivial and minor matters and that most heat is engendered by strife over non-essentials, the fact remains that the real division is at the centre. In the sphere of Christian worship, that means division over the Holy Communion service. It is in dealing with matters of dispute about the Holy Communion that Creighton consistently applies his axiom of loyalty to the principles of the Church of England. He is guided also by another axiom which is characteristically Anglican. He is ready to leave open questions open, to leave the unknown and the unknowable undefined. It is always folly to cover up inescapable ignorance by unwarrantable definition. The Church of England believed in the Real Presence of Christ in the sacrament but it did not define the mode of his presence. He writes in a private letter of 25 November 1890:

Is your brother to be confirmed as a member of the Church? Please tell him that no one believes in Transubstantiation. The Church of Rome is weighted with a doctrine which has lost all meaning, because it is connected with a system of philosophy which is no longer held: 'substance' and 'accidents' are now echoes of extinct metaphysics.

But ask him to consider that there are only two alternatives: either there is a real presence of our Blessed Lord in the Sacrament, or there is a real absence. Ask him if it is not absolute 'common sense' to a Christian to hold that the results of Christ's Incarnation are communicated to the individual soul. Tell him that the sacramental system is the only means of holding the nearness of Christ to the believers: tell him that it is a matter of fact that all bodies which reject or explain away the Sacraments drift into Unitarianism. They push our Lord farther and farther away till He is lost to their eyes.[13]

The fruitlessness of the wrangles about the 'Real Presence' is a constant theme of Creighton's teaching about the Holy Communion. Two other letters may be cited as an indication of his mind in the matter. To one correspondent he writes:

It has always seemed to me that the Church of England recognises as strongly as possible the fact of the presence in the elements at Communion, but has declined to express any opinion on the method. . . . The theology of the English Church was best expressed by Queen Elizabeth,

> 'Christ was the word and spake it:
> He took the bread and brake it,
> And what his word did make it,
> That I believe and take it.'

I think that the only point to make is that we abstain from definition on points where Scripture does not lay down a foundation.[14]

In any case the question was not so concise as is often supposed, and to another correspondent he writes:

The Church of England repudiates two views of the sacrament of the Lord's Supper, (1) that it is merely commemorative (2) that there is the change in the elements known as

F

Transubstantiation. Between these opinions any other has to be judged by its agreement with the language of the Communion Service.

You say this is a crucial question. Pardon me if I say that I wonder why people are so heated about this particular matter. The faith of Christendom is contained in the Creeds: none of them mention the Sacraments. All branches of the Catholic Church are agreed in their practice, in the nature of the rite, in the value which they assign to the Sacrament. Differences of opinion are not about the virtue received but about the mode of its reception: there is no real difference about the necessity of co-operation on the part of the recipient, i.e. the faithful reception. The difference is solely about the mode and nature of the process which precedes reception. How is this a crucial matter? It is not a matter of revelation: it is not a question asked in the early Church. It is simply the desire of man to satisfy his curiosity. Can any conclusion claim more rank than a hypothesis?

The Church of England is primitive in the sense in which early Christianity did not ask questions impossible to answer with certainty.[15]

There were many questions about the Holy Communion that were submitted to him for his opinion and advice. He thought evening Communion was to be deplored. The introduction of this by Hook, Vicar of Leeds, had made another question on which Christians can differ and the multiplication of such points of difference saddened Creighton. He advises against the introduction of Children's Eucharists because 'they accentuate a phase of our Communion service which the Church has certainly not accentuated, namely that of worship as opposed to Communion'.[16]

He would not have any truck with the demand of some tee-totallers for the use of unfermented wine. 'I know the demand and I respect their scruples. But you will observe that the whole history of the Roman Church has been that of accommodation to popular demand—leading to an obscuring of truth in the long run. To change the elements which our Lord used is a very serious matter. It is an attempt to be better and wiser than He was. If we once depart from the plain words of scripture, where are we?'[17]

The vexed question of Reservation was a bigger and more troublesome issue. Here again Creighton looks for principles on which to base his rulings and to discover and interpret the mind of the Church of England. Three principles emerge from his writings on the subject: (1) The needs of the sick should be considered rather than the convenience of the priest. (2) When used it should be regarded as an extension of the service in church. (3) There should be no Reservation in church. Creighton's considered views were set out in a letter to his Suffragan Bishop of Stepney (Winnington Ingram).

It is clear that the Prayer Book contemplates the good of the sick person, and provides that he should have the satisfaction of a complete service, including Consecration, in his presence. Reservation in any form upsets this, and substitutes the convenience of the priest as the determining element in the case. This is the main point to be considered. The priest must not consider his own convenience till he is driven by absolute stress to do so. Of course population has vastly increased, and also the desire of sick persons for frequent Communion. If the demand is beyond the power of the staff to supply, then it may be permissible to carry the Sacrament to sick people after a Celebration in Church, if they request it, and have a complete Celebration at home when possible. But I think it should be remembered (1) that great Festivals have Octaves, and that the sick may be provided for during the Octave; (2) if this is not enough, the administration to the sick should be as far as possible a continuation of the service in church, and should follow upon it. My opinion is that the whole matter should be as rare as possible: that it should be regarded as an inevitable necessity, not part of a system; that there should be no definite reservation in church, but that it be a supplement outside to a service performed inside.

This is my own opinion on a reasonable survey of the case. The difficulty in applying it is that men are rarely reasonable, and if recognised as such hasten to become unreasonable.[18]

A further statement of his views is contained in a letter to one of his clergy:

The Prayer Book of 1549 allowed the Communion to be carried directly from church on days when there was a Celebration, to sick persons who gave notice. Otherwise the consecration was to take place in their room as at present. There was no question of any general reservation in church for an emergency. This restricted form of reservation was struck out in 1552 and has never been restored. Moreover a rubric was added: 'It shall never be carried out of the church.' I know the attempts to explain that away, but we must not try to explain away plain words, which have to be read in the light of the previous concession. It is impossible to avoid the conclusion that the intention was:

(1) That the recipient should be solely considered, and that the Consecration in his presence was thought a desirable part of the service;

(2) That provision for exceptional cases was made by the rubric about spiritual Communion:

(3) That the strong intention was to prevent the growth of a mechanical conception of the efficacy of the Sacraments.

I very seriously think that we must all accept these conclusions: and I am sure that our ministrations will be helped by so doing.[19]

Creighton's dislike of the practice of Reservation was inevitable in a man who believed so strongly in the wisdom of the mind and intention of the Church of England in the matter, so unequivocally set out in the Prayer Book. He appreciated the practical pastoral problem arising from the increase in population and from the practice of more frequent Communions. He set supreme value on the Holy Communion and rejoiced that it was celebrated more frequently and more reverently than ever before. But the more he reflected on the question of Reservation the more he was persuaded of the soundness of the Prayer Book position. He believed that deviations from it would lead to excesses and that reservation for the sick would lead to reservation for adoration and so to Benediction. There was also a theological issue at stake. The Prayer Book was a bulwark against a mechanical view of the sacrament, and the danger of such a view prevailing had not passed. No plea could therefore be sustained on the ground that abuses would not now arise. 'The plain fact is that the wisdom of the framers of the Prayer Book is amply justified. This has to be faced. No Bishop could say publicly that he believed reservation for the sick to be absolutely free from danger of any ulterior results.'[20]

One of the questions on which Creighton as Bishop was consulted from time to time was the admission of nonconformists to the Holy Communion of the Church of England. In his handling of this question he reveals his devotion to freedom and charity combined with a love of order and a respect for regulation. The principle by which this question was resolved was the principle of Christian courtesy. On this principle nonconformists could be admitted to Holy Communion in the Church of England. The Church's own rules were for her own members. But the Prayer Book did not contemplate the presence of nonconformists at home or members of other religious communities abroad. Such cases, when they arose, required special consideration. Among those who consulted Creighton for guidance on this point was the Assistant Bishop in Northern and Central Europe, to whom Creighton writes:

The decision will depend on the place we make in ecclesiastical organisation for *Christian courtesy*. How ought we to recognise this undoubted virtue? Is it not the point from which we ought to start in working for union? It seems to me that our relations to the Eastern and Western Church are different owing to their different attitudes on this point. The

Roman Church is discourteous; the Greek Church is courteous. We are freer and broader than either, and can go further. An Anglican wishes to communicate, without ceasing to be an Anglican, with either East or West. He sees no insuperable difficulties in the way. He practically asks that the settlement of his own ecclesiastical position be left to himself, but that it be courteously recognised by other bodies, without any departure on their side from their own basis. This is the first step towards reunion. How are we to ask and not give? We have never declared against Lutherans and Presbyterians. Their system differs from ours, and we do not agree with it. But if a Lutheran or a Presbyterian is in a position where he can only attend our services, where he does so and where he wishes to be a communicant, I am in favour of admitting him as a *matter of courtesy*. We are not responsible for him, but we may allow him to use our services on his own responsibility. This does not affect our discipline to our own people—and does not come under the Rubric at all. It is an exceptional case which altered circumstances have created.

I may say that this was the opinion of the late Archbishop [Dr. Benson] with whom I talked on this subject. I should be very glad if you could take the same view, as I believe that the establishment of this principle would be a real help in our dealings with other Communions.[21]

Creighton, who always left his clergy the maximum freedom of discretion, took the view that this question of the admission to Holy Communion of those who were not members of the Church of England was a matter for the Bishop to decide.

It is a question of Christian courtesy, and has to be decided by consideration of the position of the Church of England. We are not a proselytising body: we do not claim that salvation is only possible within our system. We have our system and our discipline for our own people. The question is: Do we stand aloof from all others? This cannot be settled by individual priests. It is a matter for the bishops. It has been frequently discussed by them. I have heard the opinion of Archbishop Benson and of the present Archbishop. They agreed—and so do I—that the Church of England may allow its services to be used by members of other communions at their own responsibility, as a matter of Christian courtesy, not of right. There is no principle involved in this, except the principle of Christian charity. Let the Church of Rome disregard this in the supposed interest of its own organisation: but we will not be so foolish or so narrow as to follow their example. The clergy have no responsibility in the matter. Members of other Communions ask if they may use their ministrations, and use their altars: my answer is yes, they may do so at their own responsibility: you simply lend them your services. I take the responsibility of admitting them. This is a matter outside your discretion: it is my business, not yours. I give the same directions in England and outside England. It is not the function of the individual priest to define the position of the Church of England; it is the function of the Bishop.[22]

On all questions of admission to Holy Communion Creighton's decisions are large-hearted, not soft-hearted. He was by instinct magnanimous, never sentimental. It was his consistent search for principle that raised his judgements above the level of mere kindliness. In none of his judgements was he looking for the easy way out. Every decision was carefully weighed but when problems were complex and intricate and admitted of no easy solution the scales were always tipped on the side of charity. There were times when no charity was called for, when the issue was crystal clear and allowed of no ambiguity. The refusal of Communion was a serious matter and required unequivocal grounds before such a grave step could be taken. When he received a complaint that persons had been refused Communion in a certain church because they would not make their confession previously, the Bishop replied with instantaneous ease.

The grounds on which a clergyman may refuse Holy Communion to a parishioner are laid down in the rubric before

the Communion Office. These grounds in each case require
public notoriety of the offence for which the refusal is made.

It is not in a clergyman's power to use his duty of admin-
istering the Holy Communion as a means of enforcing his
own ideas of ecclesiastical discipline. He may advise such
form of preparation as he thinks best: he can enforce none:
the exact method of preparation is left by the Church of
England to the individual conscience.

Refusal of Holy Communion is a judicial decision pronounced on the character of the person to whom it is
refused. In each case the clergyman is bound to inform the
Ordinary, who is the real judge. The power of the individual
clergyman is merely suspensory, pending a proper decision.

Any form of excommunication is a charge that the person
excommunicated is a 'notorious evil-liver'. Such a charge can
be brought before the cognisance of a civil court: if it
cannot be fully proved, it is a libel.[23]

Creighton was always seeking to keep the door of the Church
wide open. He knew that the door of Heaven was wider than
the door of the Church, that good order required rules, and that
some rules would be necessarily restrictive. The Church was
not a free-for-all society, but it was important not to multiply
restrictive rules and to recognize that the Church of England
had abrogated some of the older rules. One of the rules that the
Church of England had abrogated was the rule of fasting before
Communion. On this subject he made one of his rare inter-
ventions at Convocation. In answer to the contention that the
rule of compulsory fast had never been abrogated, Creighton
pointed out how grave would be 'the limitation of the practical
power of the Church of England as an independent branch of
the Catholic Church if we were to admit that the practice of
the Church since the sixteenth century did not in itself establish
an abrogation of customs which before that time had been in
use'.[24] To enforce fasting Communion was a needless source of
division and irritation. It ignored the changed circumstances
of life and seemed to Creighton lacking in common sense. 'By

calling a custom a Catholic custom you do not exempt it from the necessity of reasonable explanation.'[25] *Autres temps, autres mœurs*, was his simple view of the matter.

Creighton's desire to keep the door of the Church wide open can also be seen in the advice he gave to the clergy on questions raised by them in connexion with the administration of baptism. In answer to a question as to what a clergyman should do who had been asked by a Presbyterian living in his parish, a small country village, to baptize his child with the stipulation that the child should not be brought into the English Church, he replies:

> The case which you bring before me does not seem to me to fall under the Rubric which was framed in view only of members of our Church, and prescribes the normal proceeding towards them.
>
> You are not asked to officiate as a clergyman towards members of your own Church: but you are asked to perform a rite for those who are not under your spiritual jurisdiction, to help them in fact, in an emergency.
>
> Such a matter is in your discretion. Baptism is a rite of almost every religious body; it may be performed by a layman in case of necessity. In this instance you are asked to perform it, not as a Priest of the Church of England, but as a minister of religion. It is something outside your official duty and not governed by the same rules. Public baptism involves both baptism and reception into the Church of England. I do not see any reason why, in your capacity as a spiritual person, you should not perform the first part privately, though you are not requested to do the second publicly. It is in itself important that a child should be baptized into Christ's Church; and I should be inclined to baptize anyone who applied, on grounds of Christian charity.[26]

He reminds another clergyman, who asks a question about a child baptized by a Roman Catholic priest, that baptism is into the universal Church of Christ and not into any particular branch of it. The question of the reception of such a child into the Church of England does not, therefore, arise:

> The form of reception in the Prayer Book is into the congregation of Christ's flock, i.e. into the Universal Church of Christ, which is apart from and beyond differences such as exist between the Church of England and the Church of Rome. There is no form of reception for a child into the Church of England as such, and I do not think such a form necessary. I, therefore, cannot advise you to use the Prayer Book form in this sense.

> But this is to be remembered. Baptism is into Christ's Church—not into the Roman branch of it. The fact that the child has been baptized by a Roman priest establishes no claim that it should be brought up according to Roman teaching. It is just as much a member of Christ. The father can decide with perfect freedom which communion it is to belong to, and what tenets it is to be taught.[27]

Rules are good servants but bad masters and in all his pastoral administration on questions of baptism Creighton reminded his clergy of the overriding rule—the rule of charity.

> It is an obligation in a parish priest to baptize all presented from his parish. It is an act of Christian charity to baptize any who are brought for baptism and not to refer them elsewhere lest they feel discouraged by technical rules of which they are unaware. The same Christian charity grants baptism without the proper number of sponsors in cases of difficulty. Really the sponsors represent the body of the faithful, and we hope that in a Christian land the organization of the Church will supply the teaching which it is the duty of the sponsors to promise.[28]

'The marriage question is dreadfully difficult and would require a volume.' So wrote Creighton to one of his clergy. There was no pastoral problem that he found more difficult and his views are not completely consistent. The question is usually raised in connexion with re-marriage after divorce. Creighton's policy was to leave his clergy complete freedom in deciding whether a re-marriage after divorce, when the former partner was still living, should take place in church. He would advise, when asked to do so, but would leave the decision to the incumbent's discretion: 'It is entirely at your discretion to perform the marriage service for the innocent party of a divorce. I have no orders to give in such a matter, when you have personal knowledge which you are justified in acting upon.'[29]

In general Creighton seems always to have been ready to leave the matter in the hands of the person best able to judge the particular circumstances. He was aware of the difficulty of using the Prayer Book Service for a second time while a former partner was still living:

> The advice which I always give in the case of re-marriage of a divorced person is: Inasmuch as it is legal, in the case of the innocent party the Church leaves it to his or her conscience to decide. But the Church Service is drawn up for normal not for abnormal cases, to which it does not strictly apply. The Civil Contract should suffice.
>
> I admit that in this case the re-marriage of the guilty husband leaves the wife practically a widow. You might hold this view and regard her as such. But this would not be known generally and all such marriages in Church create comment.
>
> I can only lay down general principles and leave the decision to your discretion with a fuller knowledge of the circumstances.[30]

Creighton's views are set out more extensively in a speech in Convocation on 7 July 1897, in presenting the report of a Convocation Committee on divorce:

> It is extraordinary how complicated and difficult the consideration of this question is. It is a point upon which, perhaps more than any other, we feel the difference between the medieval and the modern mind. It would be almost true to say that all through the Middle Ages the tendency of men was to wish to have things clearly and logically put upon

paper; that they were more concerned in expressing lofty principles as such than they were concerned in carrying out those principles in action. . . . Nowadays we are all practical certainly to this extent, that our desire is that the laws should be carried out, and that they should represent what is the popular conscience at the time at which they are passed . . . attempts to take the letter of a medieval law, and to infer from it that there was a corresponding practice, are very often exceedingly misleading.

It is not that the Church at any period whatever had any doubt that marriage was indissoluble . . . but it seems to me that there is no point upon which the Western Church displayed such incompetence, for I can call it by no other name, than in its dealing with the question of marriage. The Church found exceeding difficulty and showed exceeding reluctance in defining what marriage was. Therefore, while it is perfectly true to say that a valid marriage properly contracted was indissoluble, yet during the greater part of the Middle Ages, it was almost impossible to say what a valid marriage was and how a valid marriage could be contracted. . . .

But the Church of England does not undertake to impose upon the conscience of anybody a burden which is greater than he can bear, and your committee could only go on to say that: 'If any Christian, conscientiously believing himself or herself permitted by our Lord's words to re-marry, determine to do so, we recommend that then endeavour should be made to dissuade such person from seeking marriage with the rites of the Church, legal provision having been made by civil process. . . .' The marriage service is exceedingly unsuitable to be said a second time when there is a person still alive to whom the same pledges were made . . . no one contemplating the marriage service could conceive that it was composed with a view to such a case.[31]

So far as it is possible to summarize Creighton's views on marriage and divorce we may say that he regarded Christ's teaching as the enunciation of principles, not of legislation. Particular cases should be judged on their merits by those who were in a position to know the circumstances. A final decision should be left to the clergyman concerned. The Western Church had always been muddled on the subject and the Church of England was in like case. He had written to Archbishop Benson: 'What people call "the law of the Church" became unworkable when dispensations were cut off.'[32] In any consideration of this vexed problem the overriding principle of charity should not be lost sight of. The following extract from a letter represents his most characteristic utterance on the subject:

> Speaking generally the question raises in its extremist form the problem of the actual application to life of the principles of the Gospel. We must remember—it cannot be remembered too much—that the Gospel consists of principles not of maxims. The only possible principle concerning marriage is that it is indissoluble. But all principles are set aside by sin; and our Lord recognised that as regards marriage. . . . I must own myself to a strong indisposition to set the Church against the State on such a point as the interpretation of the latitude to be assigned to the permission of dissolution which our Lord's words imply. It has always been found difficult to adjust law and equity. But is the Church on this point to admit of no equity? The medieval system was a mass of fictions or dispensations and subterfuges. The question has always troubled the English Church. Cranmer, Andrewes, Laud alike had no fixed principles. Now the State has taken the matter into its hand and marriages are primarily civil contracts. We as Christians abhor divorce: but when a divorce has been judged necessary, are we to refuse any liberty to the innocent and wronged party? It seems to me a matter for our discretion on equitable grounds in each case. I could not advise any of my clergy to refuse to solemnise a marriage of an innocent person who genuinely desired God's blessing. I prefer to err on the side of charity.[33]

7 · THE RITUAL CLOUD

'THE diocese is in great peace and nothing of any importance awaits me.' When Creighton wrote these words to the Bishop of Leicester on 30 March 1896, how little he knew that within a year he would be hurled from the comparative peace of the Peterborough diocese into the ecclesiastical maelstrom of London. It was also to bring him to his grave, and the grave-diggers were the fanatics and extremists, Protestant and Catholic, who were determined to go their own way. In number they were comparatively few. Some of them were men of great religious zeal but, as Creighton remarked, 'the excessive demands of the scruples of good men have always been dangerous'. He was soon to test the truth of his own words at the bar of his own experience.

The ritual troubles centred mainly on the use of incense and the reservation of the sacrament of Holy Communion. The vestments question had been settled by disobedience in the previous generation. Prosecution and imprisonment had won the day for the losing side. During Creighton's London episcopate, though there were still vestiarian skirmishes, the main conflict was concentrated on other issues. The ritual innovations and the revival within the Church of England of late medieval ceremonial usages, though they were the occasion of the conflict, were not the deep underlying cause of it.

The real question now raised is the maintenance of the Church of England as it has been accepted by the English people in relation to their national life during three centuries and a half. Nobody feels any interest in ceremonies as such, but they feel that a powerful and useful institution must not be turned into something which it has never been and which they do not want. Roman ways are suspected because they lead up to the Roman conception of the Church as an organization created and ruled by the clergy, existing independently of its members, conferring or withholding salvation according as its rules are observed.[1]

In these words Creighton put his finger on the real point at issue. He was always anxious to turn from the squabble about small things to the conflict of principles involved. He understood the layman's attitude to church disorders. The layman 'is uneasy and disturbed at two things: first, he has a notion that the system of the Church of England is being changed back again into the system which it is meant to reform; and, secondly, he is profoundly shocked at the appearance of clerical insubordination'.[2] Creighton saw, too, that the Englishman's devotion to liberty was at stake. 'The English people are not primarily interested in theological questions from a strictly theological point of view; but they regard with suspicion any form of theological opinion which they think even remotely threatens that idea of freedom which they rightly hold dear.'[3]

The maintenance of liberty was the crux of the matter for Creighton himself.

Priesthood, Sacraments, Confession, all are explicable by themselves. They can be placed in a system which finds room for individual liberty, or in a system which excludes it. But it makes a great difference how the system shapes itself. Do not let us make a mistake. The question to be decided is: How much of the results of the Oxford Movement are to be permanently incorporated into the Anglican system? The answer is, from my point of view: As much as is compatible with the maintenance of that system as founded on a view of the Church which safeguards liberty.[4]

The individual must be free but the institution must stand for something. A reconciliation between these two important principles must somehow be found. Unwilling as he was to hamper good men by controversy about non-essentials, Creighton felt that excessive divergencies must be restrained. But he had no wish to narrow the Church of England. His desire and his duty was to keep the Church comprehensive. At his first Diocesan Conference in London he declared his policy. 'I think it my duty as Bishop of this diocese to show my sympathy with all forms of service and all forms of religious zeal which are loyally in accordance with the principles of the Church of England.'[5]

This was the criterion to which he constantly appealed. 'I very much wish to have ecclesiastical matters raised above trivialities to a conception of the mind and intention of the English Church—the noblest exhibition of Christianity, and therefore the most difficult to maintain. The present disquiet is due to an uneasy feeling that this is being frittered away into the forms of a mechanical system, which, if it were to spread, would exercise a pernicious effect on the national character.'[6] Creighton fully recognized that there had been times when the Church of England had failed to understand its own principles, when it had been too insular, and too suspicious of the great heritage of the past. This would not be redressed by a revival of antiquarianism which undermined those principles, but by a recovery of the principles and by loyalty to them. 'We must fall into line on a liberal interpretation of the Anglican system: this must be by reference to its principles, not its letter.'[7] This was the course he was determined to pursue, without haste, without pedantry, and without coercion.

Creighton was more concerned with the Church of the twentieth century than with the Church of the sixteenth century. Reformation must be continuous. 'Progress can only be made when all that is good in the past is retained—we do not want to subvert 1559, but to absorb it, and go beyond it. . . . We may add to the wisdom of the sixteenth century, but we cannot put that away in favour of the ignorance of the fourteenth century.'[8] The positive principles of the English Reformation had to be maintained, otherwise the true temper of the Church of England would be lost. 'People mean by the principles of the Reformation those changes in the medieval system which made for liberty and for the training of the individual to a sense of his responsibility in the sight of God.

If all that was incidental and trivial were disregarded, recent controversy would be found to be concerned with two matters regarded as cardinal points at the Reformation—the restoration of the primitive conception of Holy Communion for the medieval conception of the Mass, and the abolition of the disciplinary requirement of confession as necessary before Communion.'[9]

In trying to restore some kind of liturgical order in the chaotic condition of the London diocese, Creighton exercised great patience and put all his faith in persuasion and the force of argument. His first impression of the diocese made it clear to him just how formidable his task was. 'Party spirit is stormy and antagonisms are hard to overcome. I have a general sense that everybody is trying to exploit me, and if I do not do just what they want, are prepared to abuse me. I feel it necessary to screw my head on tight and go my own way very gently.'[10] He never allowed himself to be deflected by abuse from following the only course he believed had any hope of success.

My duty is to deal with my clergy straightforwardly and frankly, to deal with them in the spirit of kindliness and in the spirit of Christian love, to deal with them by means of arguments, and not by attempting to coerce them or to bring pressure upon them to go in directions which are contrary to their own consciences. It is my duty to try to bring them all together equally into agreement upon the great fundamental points of our Christian practice, because in matters of Christian faith, of course, we are not divided. We are divided simply and solely upon matters whose importance—and I admit they are of importance—is very frequently overstated and over-estimated. It is my duty, a duty which I have constantly before me, and at no time more than at present, to try by personal persuasion and personal influence, by talking and conference with those who seem to be divided, to bring all together into an understanding at least of one another's position, that we may discover exactly what are the points upon which we differ; for until we have discovered those, any attempt at agreement is obviously quite impossible.[11]

Creighton's policy of patience and persuasion led him to work privately for peace and to shun publicity. It also involved him in repudiating any drastic action that would have pacified one side at the expense of inflaming the other. 'I always have before my eyes the advice of Gamaliel, and I am convinced that the purposes of God are not to be wrought by the wrath of man.'[12] The result of this policy was that he was distrusted and attacked by the extremists on both sides. The wing of agitators on the English Church Union side thought that he did not understand or care for the 'Catholic Church'. Creighton, for his part, thought that they did not understand or care for the Church of England. He was a profound believer in national churches. The Reformation in England was to him primarily a national movement, creating a Church in conformity with the needs and aspirations of the English people. He was out of sympathy with the extreme evangelicals because he did not wish to compel uniformity, and had a horror of anything which looked like persecution. Their violent agitation repelled him and only won sympathy for those whom Creighton was trying to bring into order. The noisy disruption of services by Kensit and his gang, and the ultra-Protestant Erastian attack led by Sir William Harcourt, made the Anglo-Catholic extremists more determined not to submit lest they might be thought to be giving in to unseemly agitators.

In the midst of it all Creighton never flinched from his duty nor would he be deflected from doing it in the way he thought right. 'My one desire is that the course which is pursued may be the largest, the wisest and the best.'[13] Perhaps he was too patient and too temperate. The Press commented on 'the airy way' in which he spoke of the matter and 'the contemptuous indifference' with which he treated the storms. The truth is that he felt it all keenly and was intensely saddened by it. 'But it is a weary world', he writes to his daughter Beatrice in October 1899; 'the incense people are now cock-a-hoop because they thought that Lord Halifax was greatly cheered [at the Church Congress, 1899] and I fear that I shall not settle them all peacefully. It is abhorrent to all my views to proceed against an excellent clergyman for his ritual: but I fear that I cannot help myself and will go down to posterity as a persecutor. Such is life'.[14]

The use of incense was not a subject Creighton could get excited about. He disliked the ceremonial use of it (the censing of persons and things) and objected to being censed himself. But Sir Lewis T. Dibdin records: 'I remember the last time I saw him he said apropos of the extremists and incense that his personal inclination was to say, "If they like to make a smell, let them." '[15] The mental attitude revealed by such a remark was not likely to satisfy either side. Creighton disliked incense because he thought it would never do in England on aesthetic grounds. 'The Italian waves his censer in a nice slovenly way which is all right; but the pomp and self-consciousness of the English acolyte seemed to me artistically offensive. The Englishman is no good for that purpose. He takes himself too seriously whatever he does.'[16] But in persuading churches to modify their use of incense, and in other cases dissuading them from introducing it, Creighton had firmer ground on which he took his stand:

> Incense raises the question of the interpretation of the Ornaments Rubric. I cannot see how any reasonable interpretation, which has the least chance of adoption, can go beyond the contention that the old ornaments were to be used so far as they could for the revised services, but the services must interpret the rubrics, not vice-versa. Incense might be used to dignify the service, as an accompaniment, not to emphasise particular parts of the service. This is the meaning of 'censing persons and things'. It introduces an element not otherwise recognised—and so is in itself an addition to the service.[17]

Creighton felt much more keenly about questions relating to the Holy Communion, and the tendency to assimilate the

English service to the Roman Mass. Some of his statements
provoked by controversy on this topic have already been given.
Complaints often reached him about the growing use of the
term 'Mass' on church notice-boards, in announcements, and
in teaching. The term 'Requiem Mass' was also being revived,
a term which he said 'implies a conception of the relation
of the departed to God which is a pious opinion not revealed in
Scripture'.[18] In deploring the revival of the long-disused term
'Mass', Creighton, as always, was concerned to safeguard the
meaning of the English Holy Communion service. It was one
of the subjects he chose to discuss in his Visitation Charge to
the London Diocese:

> This is the object which the Church of England ever pur-
> sued, to make the Holy Communion a service for the people,
> to which they came prepared to receive the gifts of grace in
> the way Jesus had appointed. Our own time has seen a fuller
> accomplishment of that object than any previous period has
> witnessed. The Holy Communion is more frequently and
> reverently celebrated and administered; there is a higher
> sense of its value, a greater recognition of its supreme
> importance in the services of the Church. It is greatly to be
> regretted that this advance towards the due appreciation of
> the mind of the Church, should be checked by anything
> which even remotely suggests a desire to return to that
> conception of the Holy Communion which was so pernicious.
> It was that conception which in the sixteenth century was
> denoted by the use of the term Mass. Of course, it may be
> said that there is nothing in a name; but when a word is
> associated with a long-standing controversy, it is a great
> mistake to attempt to revive it. Words gain a significance
> which cannot be removed. The revival of a word inevitably
> creates suspicions that what it has long been held to signify
> is being revived also. Few things have done more mischief
> than the needless use of this word, partly from a modern
> tendency towards brevity, but more from a desire to obliter-
> ate old distinctions, and to restore unity by agreement in

words when there was no corresponding agreement in the thing signified. The same desire has led to an antiquarian revival of many of the accompaniments of the Communion Service, which had been discarded as not directly appropriate to its true meaning.

It would take me a long time to discuss these even briefly; and I do not think that the time has arrived when this can profitably be done in detail. The point I wish to emphasise is, that the object of the Church of England at the Reformation was 'to turn the Mass into a Communion'.[19]

It is interesting to compare Creighton's measured words on this subject with those of two other historian bishops, Bishop Stubbs and Bishop Hensley Henson. Stubbs, in one of his Visitation Charges, made a similar appeal to his clergy:

I would beg the clergy to abstain from using the word Mass for the service of Celebrating the Holy Sacrament.

The word Mass signifies the form of Celebration which is proper to the Roman and unreformed Church of the West....

The service of our own Church contains all that is necessary for the complete Celebration, but in form and ritual it is not the same as the Roman.

Nothing in this distinction ought to be interpreted as affecting the validity, authenticity, or efficiency of either rite....

But to use the name that belongs to one particular form of rite for another form which, in all matters of form except the repetition of the words of Institution, is distinct from it, is not only inconsistent, but incompatible with truth. And when and where it is done, either with an intention of promoting discord, or with a wish to conceal differences of opinion and belief, it is altogether to be discountenanced. Of the silliness of this I prefer not to speak. On this point I would peremptorily insist; and would forbid the employment of the term absolutely, were I not apprehensive that those who are so foolish as to use it would not be wise enough to obey my injunction.[20]

Bishop Hensley Henson quotes both Stubbs and Creighton in his own comment on the use of the word Mass as a description of the Holy Communion:

> The word itself is harmless enough, though as a term for the Sacrament it is singularly inexpressive. . . . My observations through a number of years have led me to the conclusion that hardly anything perplexes and exasperates English people so much as the use of this word by the clergy. There is, indeed, nothing illegal in its use, but the unwisdom and the uncharity are apparent. The word Mass has been banished from the religious language of English Churchmen for nearly four centuries. It is never employed by our representative divines. It is unknown to the Eastern Churches. Why, then, should an English incumbent puzzle and annoy his people by printing it on the cover of his parish magazine, and using it in the pulpit and even in conversation.[21]

Confession was another subject that was prominent in the religious controversies by which Creighton was overwhelmed. Before he became a bishop he had written to a friend who had asked for his guidance:

> The question of Confession is one that is left in our Church to individual responsibility. The more I see the working of the Church of Rome, the less I believe in its elaborate machinery. The Anglican plan of laying down a minimum, and leaving room for more as each individual thinks fit, is certainly more invigorating. Moreover, in our Church, Confession can be approached in any way, varying from the mere asking of advice, or submitting questions on points of conscience, up to submission to a regular system. Further there is entire liberty in the choice of a person; and there is no obligation to continue the habit if, in one's judgment, it is not suitable to one's needs.[22]

In later years Creighton was continually troubled by clergy whose teaching on Confession broke the bounds that, in his mind, had been wisely prescribed by the English Church. It is true that he did not believe the practice would be widely adopted: 'It does not appear to me that the English people are ever likely to make an undue use of the Confessional.'[23]

Some of his clergy, however, were advocating the use of Confession as a preliminary to receiving the Holy Communion, and Creighton, therefore, includes the subject in his Visitation Charge to the London Diocese.

> It cannot be said that Confession was a matter of grave concern in the sixteenth century, despite the manifold abuses to which the system had been subject. It was regarded as a matter to be decided, not so much on theological grounds as on grounds of common sense. That some persons should require help in quieting their consciences, and should wish for an assurance of God's forgiveness, was regarded as consonant both to the facts of human nature and to the office of a minister of Christ. But that this process should be imposed as a discipline by the Church, or urged upon individuals as a necessary preliminary for receiving the Holy Sacrament, was regarded as contrary to Christian liberty.[24]

A genuine adoption of the regular practice of Confession would show a weakening of the moral fibre of the English character and for this reason Creighton believed that it would never be voluntarily accepted by English people to any wide extent. This made him the more insistent that it should not be taught to Confirmation candidates as part of the normal system of the English Church. It should not be 'urged on the young and impressionable', but 'left to the discretion of those whose minds are mature'.[25] As in other matters, Creighton tries to deal with recalcitrant clergy in this respect by keeping them within the bounds of the Prayer Book system. He writes to one of them:

> Let me put on record my requests to you this morning. (1) That you should not give to candidates for Confirmation any literature concerning Confession. (2) That you should not urge upon them Confession as a preliminary for Confirmation. (3) That you should not give them any teaching on the

subject beyond what is contained in the Book of Common Prayer.

The teaching of the Church of England about preparation for Holy Communion is clear. It prescribes:

(i) Self-examination.
(ii) Confession to God.
(iii) Restitution and satisfaction to man.

This is universal, but if anyone cannot quiet his own conscience, he may come for advice and absolution.

The important point is that the last course should be left to the individual who chooses to use it.

No clergyman in preparing candidates for Confirmation may teach that the exceptional method is normal. It is one thing to awaken the conscience, it is another thing to quiet it for someone else.[26]

Confession in the English Church was for abnormal, not for normal cases. Once this view of it was obscured it became out of proportion. 'Confession is meant to be the means of relieving a troubled conscience: it is being used as a means of awakening a dulled conscience, which it then proceeds to relieve in an unintelligent way. Advice and warning, even at regular intervals, can be given to the young without the formal apparatus of confession.'[27]

The ritualistic cloud which settled over Creighton's London episcopate impeded him in his true work as a bishop of the Church. This he conceived to be 'the promotion of zeal and energy in practical work for saving souls'. There is a note of lament, but not of self-pity, in his address to the Diocesan Conference in 1899:

If I have to interfere in small matters, if I seem to check zeal and curb enthusiasm, if I have to ask my clergy to pause, and think about the relation of their own particular position to the whole Church, it is because such things are necessary, not because I take pleasure in doing them.

But I would say this. I do not wish to command so much as to persuade. I wish to induce people to see themselves as others see them; to regard what they are doing in reference to its far-off effects on the conscience of others; to cultivate a true sense of the proportion of things; to deal more with ideas than with the clothing of ideas; to pay more attention to the reason of a thing than to its antiquity; to remember that the chief danger which besets those who are pursuing a high object is to confuse means with ends; to examine themselves very fully lest they confuse Christian zeal with the desire to have their own way, which is the characteristic of the purely natural man.[28]

The Romanizing movement of one wing of the Church offended Creighton's respect for the *via media* of Anglicanism and the uncouth opposition to it from the other wing of the Church offended all Creighton's finer feelings and made his task of mediation impossible. He was wide awake to the danger of the Romanizing movement and deprecated it more intelligently than those who opposed it more violently. He deplored the use of unnecessary Roman terminology. He drew the attention of some of the ritualists to a pamphlet issued by the ablest of the English Roman Catholics, Dr. Barry. It was a plea to the members of that Church to abandon an outdated terminology and to speak in accordance with the thought of the present day. 'Now if a Roman feels this,' Creighton wrote, 'what must he think of us who are plunging into rubbish which he is trying to get rid of?'[29] But more important and serious than words were the doctrines they signified. The real danger, in Creighton's view, was that doctrines disavowed at the Reformation were being taught as though they were integral to the English Church. Their revival threatened not only the basis of the English Church, but also the basis of the English character, and this was what Creighton deplored most of all. 'The nation exists by virtue of a particular type of character. Character is largely founded on religion. There is in some quarters an attempt to bring back religious observances of an exotic kind which do menace English character.'[30]

Creighton tried to set some reasonable limits to the deviations from the Prayer Book that could be allowed. The principle on which he tried to work was that any additional services should conform to the spirit and intention of the Prayer Book. On this principle certain additional services must clearly be excluded. He writes to all his clergy on 14 June 1898:

> Some of these [additional services] introduce doctrines not contained in the Prayer Book, e.g. Benediction, Rosary of the Virgin, Litany of the Saints, Services for the Dead, which incorporate the Romish view of Purgatory. This is serious—the most serious thing which is at the bottom of the present discontents. It upsets the type of service altogether: it disregards all the principles of the Church of England: it ostentatiously declares that the Church of England is an imperfect system, to be supplemented at each man's option from any source he thinks fit . . . with this the bishops can and ought to deal directly; it is a matter of doctrine.[31]

He also sent instructions to his clergy for Holy Week services:

> I am not prepared to sanction
>
> (1) The washing of altars.
> (2) The adoration of the Cross.
> (3) The benediction of the paschal candle.
>
> I do not forbid the distribution of palms, provided it be not part of any other service: and the prayers used are for a blessing of the people, not of the palms, which are to be used as memorials. The palms are not to be sprinkled or censed.[32]

The Church of England, he maintained, 'knows nothing of the use of Holy Water'.[33]

Many of the ritualists had little understanding of the novelties they introduced. Creighton himself was nearly always better informed about their origin and meaning. 'The use of a sacring bell belongs to a form of service in an unknown tongue and is not appropriate to a service which everyone understands.'[34] He was pained 'to see the clergy wear the foreign form of a college cap, the biretta, which was not at all English, neither was it ecclesiastical but simply academic: Why should the English borrow a foreign form of English hat?' In matters small and great he outmatched his opponents in knowledge and wisdom but that did not abate the passions of the fanatics or make the extremists more amenable.

Even so he achieved some measure of success. Many of the clergy loyally accepted his rulings even when it went against the grain. But there was a hard core whose resistance was inflamed by the militant character of the ultra-Protestant attack. There was also a genuine if misguided sincerity on the Anglo-Catholic side. A meeting of 220 incumbents of the ritualist party was held in Holborn Town Hall in January 1899. The resolutions passed at this meeting stated:

1. That by canonical obedience is meant obedience to the Canons, and to the Bishop of the Diocese calling on any individual to conform to the law, usages, customs and rites of the Church which have canonical authority.

2. That the clergy owe it to the whole Catholic Church to refuse to obey any demands which conflict with the law, usages, etc., of the Church, whether ecumenical or provincial which have canonical authority.

3. That the reservation of the Blessed Sacrament in parish churches and for the *bona fide* purpose of communicating the sick and dying, and the ceremonial use of incense being laudable practices of the whole Catholic Church, and both being included in the direction contained in the Ornaments Rubric, the right to such reservation and ceremonial use of incense cannot and must not be abandoned.[35]

The resolutions disturbed and saddened Creighton. He knew that they would raise a new storm, and that a not inconsiderable number of his clergy were prepared to be defiant. The resolutions were 'most disastrous'. 'I dare say they had a meaning but it was not obvious.' He writes to one of the clergy concerned:

Let me put the position before you as it appears to me. There have been a number of experiments made in the Church; many of them have outstripped the limits which the English people are prepared to accept.

You must admit that any methods of teaching must have

reference to those who are taught. The faith can be taught
in many ways: none is absolutely essential. Former usages
were framed with reference to their utility, which depended
on their acceptability. The resolutions passed at the meeting
seemed to ignore this primary truth. Ceremonies are made
for man, not man for ceremonies. It is just this point which
the bishop has to decide. Individual priests may say, 'I
think this or that is good for my people.' A bishop represents
the unity of the Church as a whole. This was the original
function of his office.

The resolutions practically assume that out of the vast
museum of ecclesiastical antiquities of the past, every
priest has a right to choose what he likes, and to carry it into
practice provided he can find an adequate body of people
who agree with him. This is subversive of all principles of
unity and government.

We all must recognise the true nature of our task, which is
to teach the Gospel to the English people in a way which
that people understands. It is worth while to take a great
deal of trouble to find out what this is.[36]

Creighton himself was prepared to take a great deal of
trouble in his search for an equitable solution of the problems
he faced. He was fortified by his knowledge of history and the
lessons he had drawn from it. He records what he calls 'a few
general truths of history':

1. The suppression of opinion has never succeeded in
England.

2. The history of the English Church is a history of vain
attempts to obtain peace by exclusion.

3. When we look back upon the past we sympathise with
those who were excluded, forgetting the points at issue, and
remembering only the value of liberty as a principle of our
national life.

4. There is no real force in England except the force of
public opinion. This operates on the minds of those against
whom it is directed by argument and not by coercion.

5. The bishops can do something if they are supported by public opinion. But that opinion does not strengthen their hands by abusing them for not acting when they had no opinion behind them.[37]

History also taught him that legal proceedings to enforce good order and any attempt to impose uniformity of worship were alike disastrous.

Englishmen never like to see people dealt with in a legal manner in consequence of their opinions. The bishops have come to the conclusion that a prosecution does more harm than good; that so far from putting down practices, it only gives them increased vitality. . . . The most deplorable periods in the history of the Church of England have been when attempts were made to enforce uniformity of worship. The belief in the possibility of enforcing upon a free people uniform forms and ideas has been a great evil to the Church.[38]

Herein lay Creighton's dilemma. In dealing with irregularities in the diocese his purpose and method were misunderstood. Not wishing to impose uniformity, he was charged with contemptuous indifference; not wishing to persecute or prosecute, he was charged with masterly inactivity tempered with epigram. It is not surprising that there are moments of real despondency. 'Church matters generally are as bad as can be. I do not see the way out of the present mess. The E.C.U. people have no common-sense and the other people are so violent that the moderates do not like to throw over the E.C.U. . . . I am not sure that there will not be a secession. I rather think it inevitable. We must do all we can to minimise it and make it unreasonable.'[39]

Difficulties were increased by a clash not only of opinions but of temperaments. A reasonable man was dealing with unreasonable men and unscrupulous methods were used. Confidential communication was impossible because the Bishop's letters were continually being published. Again, he complains: 'It is worth while noting that the difficulty of a Bishop of London in dealing in a friendly way with his clergy is enormous. If he writes a letter it is at once forwarded to the E.C.U. office, is filed for everyone to see, and he is said to have sanctioned universally something which in a particular case he is prepared to overlook. If he has a friendly talk, it is at once misrepresented in any form from which most capital may be made.'[40]

On the Protestant side Kensit was a continual thorn in the flesh. Creighton writes to him: 'Human wisdom as well as Christian charity prescribes tenderness and patience in dealing with conscientious convictions. I regret that the tone of your letter implies that neither wisdom nor charity has any place in your consideration.'[41] Sir William Harcourt was the other Protestant adversary-in-chief. His speciality was letters to *The Times*, calling on the bishops to dragoon the clergy into obedience and into uniformity. Creighton writes to Harcourt: 'I rank you with Lord Halifax. He is pursuing a revival of old methods of religious thought; you are for the old means of persecuting him. I am so far modern that I do not believe in the vitality of his ideas, or in your mode of suppressing him. I want to drag him into the light and slay him in the open. My interest is more with the Church of the twentieth century than with that even of the sixteenth.'[42]

Creighton's patient, private, firm but friendly methods of paternal episcopal administration achieved much, but not enough. He knew, to cite his own saying, that the administrator has to drive the coach while his critics are always urging him to upset it. Once he was mobbed coming out of a church in Bethnal Green: 'I have to go my way and be abused by people who want to stamp on someone else or rather want me to stamp for them.'[43] He could change neither his objectives, for they were at the very root of his being as an English churchman, nor his method of pursuing them, for this too was his very soul. Lytton Strachey, for all his scathing, saw this. Creighton, he says, 'was never a persecutor; his great practical intelligence prevented that. Firmly fixed in the English tradition of common sense, compromise and comprehension, he held on his way amid the shrieking of extremists with imperturbable moderation.'[44]

He had no yearning to play the role of inquisitor. Addressing his Diocesan Conference in the last year of his life, he made his position plain. 'I smile constantly when I open my letters and find myself earnestly entreated to suppress or put down immediately by return of post particular things and particular persons, or to remove them elsewhere. I am surprised at the readiness, which, I am sorry to say, seems to exist in the minds of some people, to reinstate the Inquisition and to clothe the Bishop of London with the powers of Inquisitor-General. I can only say that I do not believe in the Inquisition, and that there is no post which I would less willingly occupy than that of Inquisitor.'[45] One of his last acts was to veto the proposed prosecution of two of his clergy under the Clergy Discipline Measure of 1840. The charge was brought by a certain Colonel Porcelli, who gave for his address a London club. Creighton, acutely conscious of his constitutional duty and therefore aware that he could not invoke his episcopal veto lightly, was immensely relieved when he found a good reason for exercising his veto on the ground that the complainant was not a parishioner of either of the clergy concerned.

There were, therefore, no prosecutions during Creighton's episcopate. To that extent he succeeded in standing up to the Protestant fanatics. But he failed to restore the harmony and peace for which he strove. Many abuses were dropped, and some that would have arisen were not introduced, but the moderate Bishop left the extremists on both sides unappeased. It was a noble failure, and the tribute of a prominent High Churchman (Dr. Cobb), at one time Secretary of the English Church Union, underlines the nobility of it:

What rendered him a sphinx to zealots was the perfect balance of his mind, reflecting as it did the studied moderation of the Church of England. Not understanding this, the one party accused him of ignorance of what Catholicism involved, his only fault really being that he knew only too well: while the other party insisted, in language more forcible than proper, that he was playing into the hands of Rome. In the midst of the turmoil he was the still, strong man who went his own way because he knew it to be the right way, no man making him afraid.[46]

It was a tragic failure, too, for 'this dispute had robbed the Church of England of one of the wisest and greatest of her bishops, for there can be little doubt that attempts to deal with it had shortened the life of Creighton'.[47]

It was tragic also in another sense, for as Creighton said in his London Visitation Charge: 'With the cry sounding in our ears, "Arise, shine", how can we waste time by disputing about the shape of our lanterns?'[48]

8 · THE ADMIRABLE CREIGHTON

'I THINK that the late Bishop of London was perhaps the most alert and universal intelligence that existed in this land at the time of his death.'[1] Such was the tribute paid to Creighton by Lord Rosebery, and it was no empty panegyric. Even the sardonic Lytton Strachey, for all his strictures, recognized Creighton's eminence in the line of Anglican worthies. The characteristic virtues of Anglicanism, he maintained, were of a secular kind, those of scholarship or of administrative energy. 'Mandell Creighton was (perhaps) the last of a long line. Perhaps; for who can tell? It is difficult to believe that a man of Creighton's attainments will ever again be Bishop of London. . . . In Creighton, *both* the great qualities of Anglican tradition were present to a remarkable degree. It would be hard to say whether he were more distinguished as a scholar or man of affairs.'[2]

In some ways Creighton's alert mind and universal intelligence was a barrier between him and his episcopal colleagues. 'He's too clever', chuckled Archbishop Frederick Temple as Creighton was making one of his welcome after-dinner speeches at the Mansion House. That is the impression he often made, but it was not an impression to endear him to those who were not so clever or to bring him into really close harmony either with his peers or with the populace. So the dull and solemn thought him flippant and the shallow thought him insincere. Some thought him worldly.

One of the impressions that emerges from a study of his life is the lack of any real intimacy with his ecclesiastical colleagues. Randall Davidson, who was consecrated Bishop on the same day as Creighton, and who succeeded Frederick Temple as Archbishop of Canterbury, had known Creighton from undergraduate days at Oxford. Creighton's was one of the names that Randall Davidson submitted to Queen Victoria for succession to the Primacy on the death of Archbishop Benson. The two men thus knew each other over many years. Davidson was not lacking in admiration for Creighton's most obvious gifts, but he was unaware of the more spiritual qualities and the depth of his character. Commenting on Creighton's work as Bishop of London, Davidson observes:

In the duties of that Bishopric his versatilities had full play; his extraordinary readiness and thoughtful understanding, and suggestive speech, enabled him to go from place to place on the same day and say something at each which was worth hearing; and few gifts other than the purely spiritual ones would be so valuable as these to a Bishop of London.

He managed his correspondence in a curiously rapid and even airy way, and seemed to keep himself abreast of everything. He was certainly strangely unlike what any other Bishop of London had been, or is ever likely to be. A great many people who knew him well found it difficult not to believe him to be a cynic, and there were those who doubted his real hold upon the dogmatic side of Christianity. This last was probably due to his endeavour, mistaken and unsuccessful as I think it was, to appear as a finished man of the world with social experience and social gifts, who could meet other men of the world on equal terms. My personal belief is that he damaged rather than aided his real influence by this attitude, and it certainly laid him open to the misinterpretations which were widespread.[3]

It was not until Mrs. Creighton's biography was published that Davidson appreciated his life-long friend at his true worth. 'I know of no instance', he writes, 'in which the publication of a public man's biography has so greatly raised him in the estimation of good and thoughtful people.' Davidson only knew the glittering, polished, clever Creighton until the inner man was revealed in all those amazing letters of spiritual counsel and advice that adorned the biography. Davidson says: 'I never failed to learn much from my intercourse with him, but I was not one of those who had really discovered or appreciated what

I now know from his *Life* to have been the deepest and best of his qualities. At the same time I found in his latter days, when I knew him best, a frequent touch of something appealing to the deeper spiritual side of things, and it always seemed to me that he had a sound appreciation of the true proportion of great things to small in the ritual controversy.'[4]

In church circles Creighton was certainly an enigmatic figure. His closest friendships were academic and literary rather than ecclesiastical. It was the historian, J. R. Thursfield, who wrote that he was 'as true, as tender, and as wise a friend as any man ever had'.[5]

The element of mystery was heightened by his aloofness, and, in turn, his aloofness was accentuated by his indifference to affection or the plaudits of the populace. He cared little for what people thought of him. He delighted in congenial company; he welcomed the society of interesting people and he shone in such a setting. He loved dining out. But with his wife and his work he could have faced the world alone. His friendships were a pleasure to him, but not a necessity. Perhaps his northern origins and character are part of the explanation.

He was a man of deep reserve in religious matters. Not wearing his heart on his sleeve, he led some to wonder whether he had a heart to wear. But his was the reserve that belonged to his Cumbrian stock. Combined with his irresponsible flippancy, his religious reserve often led him to be misunderstood.

It was a long step from the carpenter's shop in Carlisle to the maelstrom of the London bishopric and its attendant position in London society. It never really went to his head, though he played the part and at times gave the impression of playing up to the part. But there was always a depth to his sparkle; his was more than a scintillating brilliance. His grasp of great principles gave body to his paradoxes and his epigrams were more often insights than mere witticisms. He remained, what he had always been, a mixture of gaiety and gravity. His gaiety often bordered on impish levity, but he never lost his essential seriousness of mind and purpose. He frequently remarked that happiness depended on goodness.

In his essential seriousness of mind and purpose he was a true and typical Victorian. He lived through the hey-day of the gospel of progress and he was influenced by it, though he never subscribed to its naïve optimism. For Creighton national progress is bound up with moral and spiritual religion. Speaking of youth growing up in the world, he says:

He ceases to be impressed with man's successes; he sees, perhaps too clearly, the traces of man's failures, and repines under a sense of impotence. . . . The escape from present perplexities must come from a wider outlook on the future. He must rest his faith upon the eternal power of righteousness, upon the abiding force of principles which stand above all outward organisations and are superior to any form of manifestation; upon God the supreme lawgiver of the world, God the loving Father of those who will consent to become his children, God who gives His spirit whereby the individual life may be incorporated in the spiritual order of things, which alone is real because it alone is everlasting. . . . Nations have always fallen when their material civilisation was at its height, when men trusted that the machinery of civilisation would work by its own force, and forget that all depended upon the consciousness of a national mission deep seated in the heart of individual citizens.[6]

For all his enjoyment of 'high' society and his delight in consorting with men of the world, Creighton never lost his Victorian seriousness of purpose. So, too, his familiarity with the critical and aesthetic movements of the time never weakened his grip on the Christian verities as was the case with some of his intellectual friends. The critical attack on Christianity—in full flood in his Oxford days—left him undisturbed. Preaching at a memorial service to Creighton in St. Paul's, Scott Holland was able to say:

He took his stand for God and made his great decision at the extreme hour of intellectual tension when the panic roused by the new criticism was at its height, and when the victorious efficacy of the scientific and critical methods appeared to have swept the field. It is difficult for us now to gauge the dismay of that bad hour. At the close of the sixties it seemed to us at Oxford almost incredible that a young don of any intellectual reputation for modernity should be on the Christian side. And Creighton by temperament lay open to the full force of the prevailing movement. No one could be more acutely sensitive to all that the critical spirit had to say. No one lent himself more freely to the aesthetic and other non-Christian influences of that distracted time. Yet, in spite of the swirling flood in which he found himself plunged, his inner steadiness of thought and will kept the balance.[7]

His mind was so sane, his judgement so sober, that he was not likely to be a victim of the deceptive optimism of his time. At times, however, he gives the impression of placing too much faith in the power of education to ease the lot of man and to provide a panacea for human ills. He had a lifelong interest in education, was a staunch supporter of denominational schools, took an active part in promoting the cause of adult education, and never lost an opportunity of speaking on the subject to Working Men's Clubs, Co-operative Societies, and branches of the Y.M.C.A. 'Englishmen don't really believe in education, they talk about it, but they don't do much.' Creighton himself, on the other hand, was frequently encouraging all forms of adult education. Freedom and democracy depended on education for their survival. 'Unless freedom is founded on virtue it must rapidly cease to be freedom and degenerate into tyranny. Popular government is good if the people want what is right and good in itself, if they have the capacity to choose between good and evil. . . . The whole object of education is to equip them for this purpose.'[8] The sentiments are as familiar as they are praiseworthy. They amount to a truism and are not in any way exceptional in themselves. But perhaps Creighton held them with a tenacity that was uncritical, and with a passion that is suggestive of a blind spot. The natural Englishman may not be the potential paragon of common sense and enlightened virtue that Creighton imagined him to be.

Creighton said he would like his epitaph to be, 'He tried to write true history', and he certainly deserves the epitaph he desired. Professor Chadwick's appraisal must surely stand unchallenged. 'If ever a writer deserved to be awarded epithets like impartial, unbiased, unprejudiced, that writer is Creighton.'[9] He spared no pains in pursuit of accuracy and was careful in small things as in great. When he revised the brief historical sketch of English Christianity which formed a preface to the Peterborough Diocesan Chronicle he removed St. Alban and the three British bishops who are commonly supposed to have attended the Council of Arles. 'St. Alban is so mythical and the date so hard to assign that I think he can scarcely be made into an historical character.' So, too, he writes: 'In the Chronicle I would not put the names of the British bishops who are recorded as attending the Council of Arles. I cannot think they are genuine. . . . I am of the opinion that discreet silence concerning them is best.'[10] Some of the colour and the glory might depart from the story, but Creighton aimed at writing 'true history' and no other consideration mattered.

When the *English Historical Review* was founded Creighton suggested as a possible motto for it a quotation from Sir Philip Sidney: 'Not professing any art the historian, as his matter leads him, deals with all arts; which—because it carrieth the life of a lively example—it is wonderful what light it gives to the arts themselves, so as the great Civilians keep themselves with the discourses of historians.'[11] Creighton's own wide range of interests served him well in his profession as historian. But an equally important part of his equipment as an ecclesiastical historian was his liberal and enlightened Anglicanism. This is the feature which Richard Garnett underlined in his estimate of Creighton as a historian:

Other qualities being equal no one is so well placed for writing ecclesiastical history as a liberal and enlightened divine of the Church of England. The Roman Catholic historian on one side, the anti-clerical historian on the other, may be scrupulously fair in intention; but neither will be able to forget that the cause he has at heart will be helped or harmed by his labours. In the history of every Church but his own, and even of his own down to Puritan times, the Church of England divine can afford to be perfectly impartial. He may have his preferences and his aversions, but at all events he need be under no invincible bias. His Church, moreover, is not like others, isolated from the rest by peculiar doctrines or exclusive pretensions; there is no Christian community in the world with which it has not some point of contact from which a sympathetic point of view can be obtained, and which is not in some measure represented within its communion. It is the praise of Bishop Creighton to have risen to the occasion and to have manifested all the candour and equity which may be reasonably expected from the representative of a Church so fortunately placed.[12]

Creighton's reputation as a historian of 'sovereign impartiality' is secure. But his epitaph would be incomplete if it only recorded that 'He tried to write true history'. It is as expositor of the character, mission, and destiny of the Church of England that his true greatness is revealed. At times he may have been uncritically enthusiastic about the English character and too sanguine in identifying Anglicanism with the destiny of the nation. But his ardour as an Englishman and a churchman reveal the national character and the national Church at their truest and best. His constant objective was to keep the Church of England broadly based. 'Our difficulties and differences arise because we have not a sufficiently lofty conception of the destiny of the English Church. If any disaster befalls it, the record that will be written hereafter will be that English Churchmen of this our day were not sufficiently large-hearted and high-minded to recognise the greatness of the heritage which was theirs.'[13]

The prevalence of too narrow a view of the Church of England was responsible for much mischief. So, too, were the pretensions of the clerical mind. All such pretentiousness was anathema to Creighton. It distorted the gospel and alienated the laity, and in spite of all his patience it elicited Creighton's scorn. 'There is no more ludicrous sight than the man who thinks that the "Catholic Faith and Catholic practice" are locked up in his own bosom, and will submit to no authority save that of his own sweet will. Such a man fosters in others a spirit of ἀνομία (lawlessness) which is entirely contrary to the spirit of God.'[14] Disloyalty to the principles of the Church of England on the pretext of adherence to a larger conception of Christian truth was, for Creighton, merely an expression of self-willed perversity. 'The identification of what you have been doing with the "Catholic Faith" is a conspicuously English way of talking nonsense.'

As Creighton saw it, the Romanizing movement within the Church of England threatened to destroy its real character and to put in its place a conception of the Church that Englishmen had repudiated. 'The real question now raised is the mainten-ance of the Church of England as it has been accepted by the English people in relation to their national life, during three centuries and a half. . . . Roman ways are suspected because they lead up to the Roman conception of the Church as an organisation created and ruled by the clergy, existing inde-pendently of its members, conferring or withholding salvation according as its rules are observed.'[15]

Creighton was not lacking in sympathy with the sacramental system of the Church. It was in fact a necessity for his own spiritual life. Christianity was not only the most complete explanation of life but it supplied the means of living the life which it set forth. So he valued the outward form of religion and especially the sacraments. 'Without outward helps to spiritualise life, I am afraid that I for one am too feeble to get on.' Nor did he wish to impose his views on others. Patiently he laboured to secure an agreement on principle. 'It is only by the recognition of principles that we can reach peace.' One of his last acts was to bring together opposing parties for a Round Table Conference at Fulham. The purpose was not to get bogged down by tiresome discussions of legal decisions, courts, or their judgements, but to consider beliefs and the forms of their expression. Creighton deliberately took no personal part in the proceedings, nor was he so naïve as to expect concord to emerge as a rabbit out of a conjuror's hat. But he was well satisfied with the results. The conference was not intended to lead to definite resolutions but only, in the first instance, to better understanding, and this much, he believed, had been achieved.

Whether Creighton would have succeeded, had the time been granted to him, in restoring peace and order in his diocese, and thereby to the Church of England at large, is a vain question. But the opinion of J. R. Thursfield is worth recording. Creighton spoke to Thursfield in the autumn of 1899 about his difficulties in London. He said that if only he had time he thought he could surmount them. He did not despair of subduing his more rebellious clergy by patience, moderation, and sweet reasonableness, nor of bringing the extreme Protestants to a less aggressive temper by the same means. There was no bitterness in his tone, no hankering after a weak and temporizing compromise, but an infinite tenderness for the sincere convictions of men of different views, and an assured confidence that a solution and a reconciliation might be found in a better appreciation of the historical position and antecedents of the Anglican Church. 'I myself', Thursfield adds, 'never doubted that he would succeed had the time he craved been granted to him. But, alas, it was not to be. His immense powers of sympathy, his single minded devotion, his rare gifts of raising the most diverse of men to a level of thought and action far above their ordinary selves must have prevailed in the end.'[16]

Certainly Creighton himself never despaired. His dedicated devotion to the Church of England was too great for that. The future would be more splendid than the past; the latter glory of this house would be greater than the former. 'I believe it is possible that by putting before the mind of the clergy broad considerations of the character and of the destiny of the English Church, it may be quite within our power to create, perhaps for the first time in the history of that Church, a unanimity of opinion and an understanding of the great work

I

to which the providence of God has called us, which may make us strong for a fresh beginning in the annals of that Church which we all love so well.'[17]

Creighton's claim to fame as an English churchman rests ultimately on his grasp of the two principles of law and liberty. 'His cachet', writes J. N. Figgis, 'as a teacher, as a historian and as a bishop, was just this—that no one ever had a stronger sense of the value of organised government and the need of authority alike in Church and State, combined with a respect for individuality and a belief in freedom which were of the essence of the man. This, more than anything else, made him a representative of the English Church at its best, and that is of the English character at its best.'[18] In the same essay Figgis stresses Creighton's respect for the individual. 'Alike in religion, politics, learning, he always respected and believed in the individual. His great object indeed was to make the individual believe in himself.' That was the secret of his success as a teacher and it remained one of his guiding principles.

Freedom and authority were not contradictory principles. They were equally essential to the well-being of any society, be it ecclesiastical or civil. It was of the essence of the Church of England that there should be a wide latitude within it, but there must also be order. It must combine freedom for the individual with the order necessary for the maintenance of the institution. Creighton was 'an enthusiastic and fanatical Anglican', simply because he believed that the Church of England had reconciled these two essential principles more effectively than any other Christian body.

He constantly maintained that liberty was the most precious possession of man, but it was not a prize so much as a burden. One of his recurring themes was the responsibilities of liberty.

Liberty is the inalienable possession of men; liberty to express himself, to speak out his thoughts, to become all that he can become, to find scope for his powers, to develop his spiritual capacities. But there is in actual practice the difficulty of adjusting each man's claim for himself with the equally valid claim of every one of his fellows. This is the problem which society has to solve, and on its solution social well-being depends. Liberty is frequently regarded as if it were only a right; but it is also a serious responsibility. The great question for the modern world to determine is, how men are to be fitted to bear the heavy burden of liberty.[19]

Failure to recognize the value and necessity of liberty had been disastrous in the history of the Church and one of the principal causes of division within Christendom. 'The idea of a Christian Church universal in its organisation has failed because it would not make room for two forces which have been most powerful in shaping the modern world—the forces of nationality and liberty.'[20] The Church of England was the offspring of these forces, and its authority must be exercised through influence and not through power. Speaking of the work of a national Church Creighton asserted: 'It persuades rather than commands; its weapon is influence not power . . . the Church of England has the satisfaction of knowing that it is training the generations on whom the future of the world depends, and it is content to gender sons and daughters into freedom . . . it works in hope of repairing breaches and restoring ancient ways.'[21]

To work by influence rather than by power requires immense patience but it is the only method that is consonant with the Church's gospel. 'There are only two ways of dealing with religious opinions, that of Gamaliel and that of the Inquisition. I always regard Gamaliel as the first exponent of liberal opinions.'[22] In his Hulsean Lectures on *Persecution and Tolerance* Creighton had enlarged on this theme that the Church's weapons are to be found not in power but in influence. He quotes the cry of St. Bernard to Pope Eugenius IV: 'Rule that you may serve. Act up to this; and do not you, a man, affect to dominate over men, lest all injustice dominate over you. I dread no poison, no sword, so much as I dread the lust of power. In your power you are the successor not of Peter but of Constantine.'[23] The lesson of history was clear for all to see: 'Does not the

history of the Church bear record to the superior greatness of
the achievements wrought by influence over those which were
wrought by power? Who can read unmoved the story of the
foundation of the Northumbrian Church or the lives of St.
Francis and his companions? Does he feel the same charm in the
lives of Pope Gregory VII or Thomas of Canterbury? Who can
fail to see the difference between those who strove to do God's
work in God's way, and those who laboured to do God's work
in man's way.'

The lesson must be taken to heart. 'Ecclesiastical power will
never be revived, but any lingering desire after it prevents the
growth of ecclesiastical influence. God has taught us that he
works by influence not by power. He taught it in his own dealings with man; he declared it in the Incarnation. But men
would not entirely learn God's lesson, and chose their own way
instead of his. He has written his condemnation of their error in
the record of history.'[24] Creighton concludes his lectures with a
warning: 'Liberty is a tender plant and needs jealous watching.
It is always unsafe in the world, and is only secure under the
guardianship of the Church, for the Church possesses the knowledge of man's eternal destiny—which alone can justify his
claim to freedom.'[25]

Creighton knew, better than most, that the Church had
often been the enemy of liberty and to that extent it had failed
to live up to its title deeds. But he also knew that, without the
Gospel, liberty was insecure. He himself used his abundant gifts
to reconcile the right of the individual to be free with the duty of
the institution to be something. 'You know', he once wrote to a
friend, 'I have almost a craze for liberty.'[26] But there was
nothing crazy in his understanding of it. The ground of liberty
is the dignity of man and ultimately Christianity alone secured
this foundation. Liberty, as he said, 'is God's gift to those who
grasp its meaning and seek His help to use it rightly'.[27]

PRINCIPAL SOURCES

Life and Letters of Mandell Creighton by His Wife, 2 vols., 1904 (cited in Notes as *Life*).

Mrs. Creighton's Notebooks and a collection of manuscript appreciations by various contemporaries (cited as MS. Source).

WRITINGS OF CREIGHTON

The *Life* contains a complete list of Creighton's published works. The following are the principal ones referred to in the present study:

History of the Papacy from the Great Schism to the Sack of Rome, 2nd Edition, 6 vols., 1897.

Cardinal Wolsey, 1888 ('Twelve English Statesmen' Series).

Queen Elizabeth, 1896.

The Church and the Nation: Charges and Addresses, 1901.

Historical Essays and Reviews, 1902.

Historical Lectures and Addresses, 1903.

Thoughts on Education, 1903.

Persecution and Tolerance (Hulsean Lectures 1893–4), 1895.

The Heritage of the Spirit, 1896.

University and Other Sermons, 1903.

The Mind of St. Peter and Other Sermons, 1904.

Counsels for Church People.

Counsels for the Young.

'The Reformation' (in *The Church Past and Present*, edited by H. M. Gwatkin, 1900).

OTHER BOOKS AND ARTICLES

H. Scott Holland, *Personal Studies*, 1905.

J. N. Figgis, *Churches in the Modern State*, 1913.

Lytton Strachey in *Life and Letters* (edited by Desmond McCarthy), Vol. II, No. 13, June 1929.

C. Jenkins in *Church Quarterly Review*, January 1930.

M. Belgion in *Theology*, Vol. lii, No. 352, October 1949.

W. O. Chadwick, *Creighton on Luther: an Inaugural Lecture*, 1959.

NOTES

Chapter One: Life in Outline

1. *Life* I, pp. 10–11.
2. Ibid., p. 11.
3. Ibid., p. 14.
4. Ibid., p. 14.
5. H. Scott Holland, *Personal Studies*, p. 210.
6. *Life* I, p. 178.
7. *Thoughts on Education*, p. 153.
8. W. O. Chadwick, *Creighton on Luther*, p. 2.
9. *The Church and the Nation*, p. 91.
10. *Life* I, p. 325.
11. MS. Source.
12. Lytton Strachey in *Life and Letters*, Vol. II, No. 13, June 1929.
13. *Persecution and Tolerance*, p. 123.
14. Ibid., p. 137.
15. Ibid., p. 140.
16. *Life* II, p. 253.
17. Ibid., p. 390.
18. Ibid., p. 261.
19. Ibid., pp. 420–1.

Chapter Two: The Inner Man

1. MS. Source.
2. *Life* I, p. 131.
3. Ibid., p. 256.
4. Ibid., p. 343.
5. H. Festing Jones, *Life of Samuel Butler*, Vol. II, p. 176.
6. Ibid., p. 177.
7. *Life* II, p. 479.
8. Ibid., p. 507.
9. Ibid., pp. 408–9.
10. *The Heritage of the Spirit*, p. 195.
11. Ibid., p. 196.
12. *Life* II, p. 400.
13. *Thoughts on Education*, p. 138.
14. *Counsels for the Young*, p. 29.
15. *Thoughts on Education*, p. 142.
16. *Life* II, p. 414.
17. Ibid., p. 410.

Chapter Three: The Historian

1. Strachey, op. cit.
2. *Historical Lectures and Addresses*, p. 5.
3. Ibid., p. 16.
4. *Life* I, p. 376.
5. *Thoughts on Education*, p. 165.
6. *Life* II, p. 504.
7. *Church Quarterly Review*, January 1930.
8. *Life* I, pp. 264–5.
9. *English Historical Review*, Vol. II, p. 571.
10. *Life* I, p. 369.
11. Ibid., p. 372.
12. Ibid., p. 373.
13. *Thoughts on Education*, p. 167.
14. *Life* I, p. 288.
15. A. L. Rowse, *The England of Elizabeth*, p. 266.
16. *Life* I, p. 216.
17. Strachey, op. cit.

Chapter Four: The Church of England

1. *Life* I, p. 241.
2. *Historical Lectures and Addresses*, p. 117.
3. *Life* I, p. 267.
4. Ibid., p. 266.
5. *The Church and the Nation*, p. 248.
6. Ibid., p. 251.
7. *Historical Lectures and Addresses*, p. 150.
8. Ibid., p. 176.
9. *The Church and the Nation*, pp. 175–6.
10. Ibid., pp. 78–79.
11. *Counsels for Church People*, pp. 33–34.
12. *Historical Lectures and Addresses*, pp. 169, 171
13. *The Church Past and Present*, pp. 130–1.
14. *Life* II, p. 375.
15. *The Church and the Nation*, p. 165.
16. MS. Source. (Letter dated 30 March 1896.)
17. *Life* II, p. 267.
18. Ibid., p. 302.
19. *Life* I, p. 315.
20. Ibid., p. 176.
21. Ibid., p. 177.
22. Ibid., p. 178.
23. Ibid.

24. *Life* II, p. 179.
25. Ibid.
26. Ibid., p. 183.
27. Ibid., p. 185.
28. Ibid., p. 113.
29. Ibid., p. 191.
30. *Historical Lectures and Addresses*, p. 29.
31. Ibid., pp. 46–47.
32. *Life* II, p. 472.
33. Ibid., pp. 506–7.
34. Ibid., pp. 375–6.
35. Ibid., p. 442.
36. Ibid., p. 411.
37. *The Church and the Nation*, pp. 292-3.
38. *University and Other Sermons.*
39. *The Church and the Nation*, p. 197.
40. Ibid., p. 191.

Chapter Five: The Church and the Nation

1. *Life* II, p. 384.
2. H. Hensley Henson, *Bishoprick Papers*, p. 209.
3. *Oxford House Papers*, Vol. III, p. 31.
4. *Life* II, p. 98.
5. Ibid., p. 99.
6. Ibid., p. 349.
7. Ibid., p. 504.
8. J. N. Figgis, *Churches in the Modern State*, pp. 236–7.
9. Ibid., pp. 238–9.
10. *The Church and the Nation*, p. 31.
11. *Life* II, pp. 82–83.
12. *Life* I, p. 319.
13. Ibid., pp. 306–7.
14. Ibid., p. 347.
15. *Life* II, p. 453.
16. *The Church and the Nation*, p. 33.
17. Ibid., p. 34.
18. Ibid., p. 41.

Chapter Six: The Office and Work of a Bishop

1. *Life* I, p. 398.
2. Ibid., p. 414.
3. *Thoughts on Education*, p. 192.
4. *The Church and the Nation*, p. 102.

5. *Life* I, p. 400.
6. *Historical Lectures and Addresses*, p. 177.
7. Ibid., p. 185.
8. Ibid., pp. 182–3.
9. Ibid., pp. 183–4.
10. *Life* II, p. 262.
11. Ibid., p. 294.
12. *The Church and the Nation*, pp. 227–8.
13. *Life* I, p. 415.
14. *Life* II, p. 302.
15. MS. Source. (Letter dated 24 October 1898.)
16. MS. Source.
17. *Life* II, pp. 280–1.
18. Ibid., p. 310.
19. Ibid., p. 311.
20. Ibid., p. 313.
21. Ibid., p. 276.
22. Ibid., pp. 276–7.
23. Ibid., pp. 274–5.
24. Ibid., p. 490.
25. Ibid., p. 426.
26. Ibid., pp. 66–67.
27. Ibid., p. 68.
28. MS. Source. (Letter dated 21 March 1900.)
29. Ibid. (Letter dated 23 June 1898.)
30. *Life* II, p. 275.
31. Ibid., pp. 322–3.
32. Ibid., p. 69.
33. Ibid., pp. 68–69.

Chapter Seven: The Ritual Cloud

1. MS. Source. (Letter dated 3 October 1899.)
2. *The Church and the Nation*, p. 234.
3. *Life* II, p. 425.
4. Ibid., p. 378.
5. Ibid., p. 287.
6. Ibid., pp. 303–4.
7. Ibid., p. 351.
8. Ibid., p. 430.
9. Ibid., pp. 425–6.
10. Ibid., p. 235.
11. Ibid., p. 292.
12. Ibid., p. 263.

13. *Life* II, p. 262.
14. MS. Source.
15. Ibid. (See also *Life* II, p. 491.)
16. *Life* II, p. 313.
17. Ibid.
18. Ibid., p. 303.
19. *The Church and the Nation*, pp. 306–7.
20. W. Stubbs, *Visitation Charges*, pp. 325–6.
21. Henson, op. cit., p. 122.
22. *Life* I, p. 411.
23. MS. Source. (Letter dated 18 February 1899.)
24. *The Church and the Nation*, pp. 310–11.
25. Ibid., p. 314.
26. *Life* II, p. 365.
27. Ibid., p. 470.
28. *The Church and the Nation*, p. 245.
29. *Life* II, p. 294.
30. Ibid., p. 301.
31. Ibid., p. 298.
32. Ibid., p. 366.
33. *The Clergyman's Magazine*, Vol. XVIII, 1884, Paper on 'Clerical Inaccuracies'.
34. MS. Source. (Letter dated 28 January 1899.)
35. *Life* II, p. 353.
36. Ibid., p. 354.
37. Ibid., p. 357.
38. Ibid., p. 293.
39. Ibid., pp. 367–8.
40. Ibid., p. 263.
41. Ibid., p. 314.
42. Ibid., p. 450.
43. Ibid., p. 341.
44. Strachey, op. cit.
45. *The Church and the Nation*, pp. 335–6.
46. *Life* II, p. 289.
47. Elliot Binns, *The Development of English Theology*, p. 122.
48. *The Church and the Nation*, p. 323.

Chapter Eight: The Admirable Creighton

1. *Life* II, p. 465.
2. Strachey, op. cit.
3. G. K. A. Bell, *Randall Davidson*, I, pp. 358–9.
4. Ibid., I, p. 358.

5. MS. Source.
6. *Thoughts on Education*, pp. 97, 104.
7. *Life* I, p. 75.
8. Ibid., pp. 381–2.
9. *Chadwick*, op. cit., p. 15.
10. *Life* II, p. 52.
11. *Life* I, p. 338.
12. *English Historical Review*, 1901, p. 211.
13. *The Church and the Nation*, p. 285.
14. *Life* II, pp. 194–5.
15. Ibid., p. 378.
16. MS. Source.
17. *Life* II, p. 297.
18. Figgis, op. cit., pp. 239–40.
19. *The Church and the Nation*, p. 46.
20. Ibid., p. 214.
21. Ibid., p. 215.
22. *Life* II, pp. 422–3.
23. *Persecution and Tolerance*, p. 83.
24. Ibid., p. 138.
25. Ibid., p. 140.
26. *Life* II, p. 346.
27. *The Mind of St. Peter and Other Sermons*, p. 91.

INDEX

Fallows, W   G
　　Mandell Creighton and the English Church, by W. G.
Fallows.　London, New York, Oxford University Press,
1964.

　　vi, 127 p.　port.　22 cm.

　　Bibliography : p. ₁117₁

　　1. Creighton, Mandell, Bp. of London, 1843–1901.　　ɪ. Title.

BX5199.C75F3　　　　　　　　922.342　　　　　　　　64–4562

Library of Congress　　　　　　₁5₁